INSTRUCTOR'S MANUAL TO ACCOMPANY

FUNDAMENTALS OF BIOLOGICAL ANTHROPOLOGY

Second Edition

John H. Relethford

State University of New York
College at Oneonta

Mayfield Publishing Company
Mountain View, California
London • Toronto

International Standard Book Number: 1-55934-665-5

Manufactured in the United States of America
10 9 8 7 6 5 4 3 2 1

Mayfield Publishing Company
1280 Villa Street
Mountain View, California 94041

PREFACE

This manual is designed to provide basic support for the second edition of my text *Fundamentals of Biological Anthropology*. This text is an abridged version of the third edition of *The Human Species: An Introduction to Biological Anthropology*. This abridged version is designed for those instructors for which the larger version might not be appropriate. First, a shorter text may be useful for those teaching on a quarter system, or a summer session, as opposed to a 15-week semester. Second, some instructors like to assign supplemental readings, and a shorter text suits this arrangement. Third, some instructors like texts with less detail than traditional introductory texts. Finally, the shorter length of this text makes it useful in general anthropology or combined archaeology and physical anthropology courses.

Each chapter covered in this guide contains a summary of the content and objectives of the chapter and a listing of contents that is more detailed than the text's table of contents. Several topics are then listed for possible classroom discussion. Sample multiple-choice and essay questions are provided. The multiple-choice questions are also available on a computerized test bank from Mayfield Publishing.

The structure of the text, and this manual, follow my own personal concept of how the basic introductory biological anthropology course should be organized. The text is divided into four parts (I usually devote one-fourth of the course to each part). Part 1 focuses on evolutionary background, including genetics, microevolution, macroevolution, and the fossil record prior to the origin of primates. Part 2 covers primate taxonomy, behavior, and evolution, including a separate chapter devoted to humans. Part 3 deals with the fossil record of human evolution, with chapters on hominid origins, evolution of the genus *Homo* (*Homo erectus* and archaic *Homo sapiens*), and the origin of modern humans. Part 4 covers human variation, with chapters on microevolution, adaptation, health and disease, and demography. All chapters on human variation are now placed together.

There are, of course, equally valid alternative styles of organization. What works well for me may not work as well for you. I have designed the text so that alternative course structures can be used with a minimum of effort. For example, some may prefer to cover the material on human variation before the material on human evolution. In this case, the assigned readings would be: Parts 1, 2, 4, and 3.

CONTENTS

PART FOUR: HUMAN VARIATION

CHAPTER 1

THE STUDY OF BIOLOGICAL ANTHROPOLOGY

Overview

This chapter has two major objectives: (1) introduction to the nature of anthropology, including discussion of the characteristics and subfields of anthropology, and (2) an introduction to the general nature of evolutionary science, including a historical overview. The chapter concludes with a contrast of evolutionary science and "creation science."

Outline

I. What Is Anthropology?
   A. Biology and Culture
   B. Variation
   C. Evolution
   D. Adaptation
   E. The Subfields of Anthropology
      1. Cultural anthropology
      2. Anthropological archaeology
      3. Linguistic anthropology
      4. Biological anthropology

II. Science and Evolution
   A. Characteristics of Science
      1. Facts
      2. Hypotheses
      3. Theories
   B. The Development of Evolutionary Theory
      1. Pre-Darwinian thought
      2. Charles Darwin and natural selection
      3. An example of natural selection
      4. Modern evolutionary thought
   C. Evidence for Evolution
   D. Science and Religion

III. Summary

IV. Supplemental Readings

   Special Topic: Biological Anthropologists at Work

Topics for Discussion

1. How does the holistic approach of anthropology contrast with the more specialized approach of other sciences? What are the advantages and disadvantages of each approach?

2. Why does the study of human variation and evolution rely so heavily on consideration of human culture?

3. Darwin's theory of natural selection relied extensively on putting together pieces from other people's work. Discuss the general nature of scientific inquiry and how information from seemingly unrelated fields can contribute to research.

4. Discuss the "creation science" movement in terms of ongoing efforts in local communities to restructure curricula. What dangers does this pose?

For further information on "creation science" and evolutionists' responses, contact

National Center for Science Education
P.O. Box 9477
Berkeley, CA 94709-0477

World Wide Web: http://www.natcenscied.org/

Multiple-Choice Questions

Correct answers are marked with an asterisk (*). There are multiple questions for certain topics.

1. Which of the following is not a characteristic of anthropology?
    a. It is concerned with both biology and culture.
    b. It is holistic.
    c. It is concerned with human variation, evolution, and adaptation.
    *d. It focuses only on prehistoric societies.

2. One difference between anthropology and many other social sciences, such as sociology, is that anthropology is concerned with human _____ as well as human behavior.
   a. economic systems
   b. political systems
   *c. biology
   d. warfare

3. Culture, as used by an anthropologist, refers to
   a. instinctual behaviors.
   *b. learned behavior.
   c. behavior imposed by law.
   d. the arts and literature enjoyed by "high society."

4. _____ refers to the successful interaction between a population and its environment.
   a. Variation
   *b. Adaptation
   c. Holism
   d. The biocultural approach

5. Which of the following is *not* a subfield of anthropology?
   a. biological anthropology
   b. cultural anthropology
   c. geographic anthropology
   *d. anthropological archaeology

6. The subfield of anthropology that deals with the study of prehistoric and historic human cultures is
   a. biological anthropology.
   b. cultural anthropology.
   c. linguistic anthropology.
   *d. anthropological archaeology.

7. A primary tool of cultural anthropology is
   a. genetic analysis.
   *b. the comparative method.
   c. the analysis of prehistoric artifacts.
   d. comparative anatomy.

8. Biological anthropologists study
   a. the fossil record for human evolution.
   b. the behavior of monkeys and apes.
   c. the genetics of living human populations.
   *d. All of the above.

9. You often hear arguments about whether evolution is a "fact" or a "theory." Which is it?
   a. fact
   b. theory
   *c. both
   d. neither

10. In science, an explanation of observed facts is known as a
    a. theory.
    *b. hypothesis.
    c. scenario.
    d. guess.

11. In the natural sciences, a set of hypotheses that has been repeatedly tested and not rejected is referred to as a
    a. fact.
    b. testable hypothesis.
    *c. theory.
    d. model.

12. Which of the following combinations of scientist / hypothesis is correct?
    a. Cuvier / adaptive radiation
    b. Darwin / catastrophism
    c. Lamarck / natural selection
    *d. None of the above.

13. Linnaeus' formal description of living organisms is an example of
    a. the formulation of a testable hypothesis.
    *b. a taxonomy.
    c. a scientific theory.
    d. a biocultural approach.

14. Prior to the development of evolutionary thinking, the dominant view of biological variation focused on
    a. mutation as the only evolutionary force.
    b. similarities between apes and humans.
    *c. an unchanging natural world.
    d. genetic versus environmental influences on intelligence.

15. Catastrophism attempted to explain the fossil record in terms of
    *a. natural catastrophes in an area, followed by organisms moving into the area from elsewhere.
    b. a series of catastrophes brought about by a creator.
    c. extinction as the only evolutionary mechanism.
    d. the failure of some organisms to survive in a changing environment.

16. The hypothesis of acquired characteristics stated that
    *a. organisms changed during their lifetime, and would then pass these changes on to their offspring.
    b. natural selection could not operate in all cases.
    c. individual organisms have total control over their ability to survive and reproduce.
    d. evolutionary changes developed in one species could be passed on to another species.

17. Darwin's development of natural selection was influenced by the writings of the economist Thomas Malthus, who noted that
    a. species change as their environment changes.
    b. there is a great deal of variation in nature.
    *c. many organisms will not survive to adulthood.
    d. economic competition is analogous to "survival of the fittest."

18. Darwin was not the only person to develop the idea of natural selection. Who was the other person?
    a. Jean-Baptiste Lamarck
    b. Thomas Huxley
    *c. Alfred Russel Wallace
    d. Georges Cuvier

19. Who wrote *On the Origin of Species by Means of Natural Selection*, the classic work providing the foundation for the development of modern evolutionary thought?
    a. Georges Cuvier
    *b. Charles Darwin
    c. Jean-Baptiste Lamarck
    d. Thomas Malthus

20. The study of evolution of the peppered moth provides an excellent example of
    a. extinction.
    b. acquired characteristics.
    *c. natural selection.
    d. migration.

21. The peppered moth in England changed in color from almost all being light-colored to almost all being dark-colored. This change was related to a changing environment, specifically
    *a. industrial pollution.
    b. the climate becoming colder.
    c. the climate becoming hotter.
    d. intensive logging of the forests.

22. Evidence for evolution consists of
    a. the fossil record.
    b. comparative anatomy.
    c. comparative genetics.
    *d. All of the above.

23. The "Scopes Monkey Trial" was about
    *a. teaching evolution in public schools.
    b. teaching creationism in public schools.
    c. teaching evolution in private schools.
    d. teaching creationism in private schools.

24. The claims of "creation science" are invalid from a *scientific* standpoint because
    *a. they propose hypotheses that cannot be tested.
    b. they violate separation of church and state.
    c. there is a scientific conspiracy against creationists.
    d. All of the above.

25. From a *legal* perspective, the "equal time" laws are flawed because
    a. they propose hypotheses that cannot be tested.
    *b. they violate separation of church and state.
    c. they have not been voted on by all citizens in a public referendum.
    d. they are state laws, and such laws must be passed at the federal level.

Essay Questions

26. What is the key difference between the evolutionary hypotheses of Lamarck and Darwin?

27. Malthus' work was critical to Darwin's development of the theory of natural selection. Summarize briefly the findings of Malthus' work and how it relates to the theory of natural selection.

CHAPTER 2

HUMAN GENETICS

Overview

The purpose of this chapter is to provide a brief background in molecular and Mendelian genetics necessary for an understanding of the evolutionary process. As such, the emphasis on molecular genetics is on the concept of information transmission (cell to cell, parent to child) and less on the actual biochemistry. Mendelian genetics is approached in a similar fashion, emphasizing basic principles of inheritance. While examples are drawn from familiar discrete traits, attention is also given to the genetics of complex traits. Mutations are discussed in terms of "errors" in information transmission. A primer on cell biology is provided at the end of the chapter, providing greater information if desired on cell structure, mitosis, and meiosis.

Outline

I. Molecular Genetics
   A. DNA: The Genetic Code
      1. The structure of DNA
      2. Functions of DNA
   B. Chromosomes and Genes
      1. Genes
      2. Mitosis and meiosis

II. Mendelian Genetics
   A. Genotypes and Phenotypes
      1. Mendel's Law of Segregation
      2. Dominant and recessive alleles
      3. Codominant alleles
   B. Predicting Offspring Distributions
   C. Chromosomes and Inheritance
      1. Mendel's Law of Independent Assortment
      2. Linkage
      3. Crossing over
      4. Sex chromosomes and sex determination
   D. The Genetics of Complex Physical Traits

III. Mutations
   A. Evolutionary Significance of Mutations
   B. Types of Mutations
   C. Rates of Mutations

IV. Summary

V. Supplemental Readings

VI. Cell Biology: A Review

   Special Topic: PCR and Ancient DNA

Topics for Discussion

1. Why is the argument over genetics or environment essentially a useless one when discussing many aspects of human biology and behavior?

2. How is the process of genetic inheritance similar to other types of information transmission (e.g., telecommunications)?

3. What would happen to a species if there were no mutations?

4. Discuss the nature-nurture debate in light of current speculations regarding the biological basis of homosexuality.

Multiple-Choice Questions

Correct answers are marked with an asterisk (*). There are multiple questions for certain topics.

1. The field of genetics concerned with the laws of inheritance is known as _____ genetics.
   a. molecular
   *b. Mendelian
   c. population
   d. evolutionary

2. The shape of a DNA molecule is a
   *a. helix.
   b. circle.
   c. elongated loop.
   d. straight line.

3. The DNA molecule contains _____ chemical bases.
   a. 1
   b. 2
   c. 3
   *d. 4

4. Each amino acid is coded for by _____ chemical bases.
   a. 1
   b. 2
   *c. 3
   d. 4

5. In DNA, the base A pairs with the base ___.
   a. C
   b. G
   *c. T
   d. X

6. DNA regulates the process of protein synthesis with the help of
   a. water.
   b. sunlight.
   *c. RNA.
   d. a variety of body salts.

7. One chemical difference between DNA and RNA is that RNA has the base ___ instead of the base T.
   a. E
   b. K
   c. S
   *d. U

8. _____ is responsible for transporting genetic information to the site of protein synthesis.
   a. Messenger DNA
   b. Transfer DNA
   *c. Messenger RNA
   d. Transfer RNA

9. Human beings have ____ pairs of chromosomes.
   a. 3
   b. 4
   *c. 23
   d. 24

10. Where is DNA found in a cell?
    a. Only in the nucleus.
    b. Only in the mitochondrion.
    *c. Mostly in the nucleus, with a small amount in the mitochondrion.
    d. Mostly in the mitochondrion, with a small amount in the nucleus.

11. The polymerase chain reaction (PCR) is used for
    a. the production of sex cells.
    b. the production of body cells.
    c. transmitting genetic information to the site of protein synthesis.
    *d. amplifying small amounts of DNA for analysis.

12. Given that humans and apes share over 98 percent of their genetic material, it seems likely that their anatomical differences involve differences in _____ genes.
    a. structural
    *b. regulatory
    c. hemoglobin
    d. jumping

13. The lack of teeth in birds and the occasional discovery of horses with three toes are two observations that provide insight into the action of
    a. meiosis.
    b. crossing-over.
    c. pleiotropic effects.
    *d. regulatory genes.

14. _____ is the production of body cells, whereas _____ is the production of sex cells.
    a. Meiosis / mitosis
    *b. Mitosis / meiosis
    c. Crossing-over / mitosis
    d. Crossing-over / meiosis

15. Humans have 23 *pairs* of chromosomes. The process of sex-cell formation provides _____ chromosomes to an offspring from *each* parent.
    a. 12
    b. 13
    *c. 23
    d. 46

16. _____ first demonstrated the principles of genetic inheritance.
    a. Charles Darwin
    *b. Gregor Mendel
    c. James Watson and Francis Crick
    d. Georges Cuvier

17. The alternative forms of a gene found at a given locus are known as
    *a. alleles.
    b. dominants.
    c. polymorphisms.
    d. polygenes.

18. Each parent contributes one allele at each locus to their offspring. This is known as the Law of
    *a. Segregation.
    b. Independent Assortment.
    c. Polygenic Inheritance.
    d. Dominance.

19. The genetic makeup of an individual is known as the
    a. phenotype.
    *b. genotype.
    c. alleles.
    d. polymorphism.

20. An allele is _____ if it masks the effect of another allele.
    a. a mutation
    b. recessive
    *c. dominant
    d. codominant

21. Mendel's experiments with pea plants showed that crossing plants with yellow seeds with plants with green seeds produced offspring with yellow seeds. This finding illustrates the principle of
    a. codominance.
    *b. dominance.
    c. mutation.
    d. crossing-over.

22. Alleles are _____ if both of their effects are shown in the phenotype.
    a. regulatory
    b. recessive
    c. dominant
    *d. codominant

11

23. Imagine a species where there is a locus with two alleles, *A* and *B*. Further imagine that *A* and *B* are codominant. How many different *phenotypes* are possible in this species?
   a. 1
   b. 2
   *c. 3
   d. 4

24. Imagine a species where there is a locus with two alleles, *A* and *B*. Further imagine that *A* is dominant and *B* is recessive. How many different *phenotypes* are possible in this species?
   a. 1
   *b. 2
   c. 3
   d. 4

25. There are two alleles for the PTC-tasting locus in humans: *T*, which codes for tasting, and *t*, which codes for non-tasting. *T* is dominant and *t* is recessive. Imagine two parents that are tasters have a child that is a non-taster. Given this information, you know that the genotypes of the parents had to have been
   *a. *Tt* and *Tt*.
   b. *TT* and *Tt*.
   c. *Tt* and *TT*.
   d. *TT* and *TT*.

26. Imagine there is a locus with two alleles, *H* and *h*, where *H* is dominant and is the "hairy nose" allele. If a man with genotype *HH* mates with a woman with genotype *hh*, the proportion of offspring expected to have the "hairy nose" *phenotype* is
   a. 25 percent.
   b. 50 percent.
   c. 75 percent.
   *d. 100 percent.

27. Imagine there is a locus with two alleles, *R* and *r*, where *R* is dominant and is the "red toe" allele. If a woman with genotype *Rr* mates with a man with genotype *Rr*, the proportion of offspring expected to have the "red toe" *phenotype* is
   a. 25 percent.
   b. 50 percent.
   *c. 75 percent.
   d. 100 percent.

28. Assume a locus with two alleles, *F* and *G*. If a woman with genotype *FG* mates with a man with genotype *FG*, the expected proportion of *heterozygotes* among their offspring is
    a. 25 percent.
    *b. 50 percent.
    c. 75 percent.
    d. 100 percent

29. Assume a locus with two alleles, *D* and *d*. If a man with genotype *Dd* mates with a woman with genotype *dd*, the expected proportion of *homozygotes* among their offspring is
    a. 25 percent.
    *b. 50 percent.
    c. 75 percent.
    d. 100 percent.

30. The *ABO* blood group has three alleles (*A, B, O*). If a woman with genotype *AO* mates with a man with genotype *BB*, the expected proportion of *heterozygotes* among their offspring is
    a. 25 percent.
    b. 50 percent.
    c. 75 percent.
    *d. 100 percent.

31. The *ABO* blood group has three alleles (*A, B, O*) where *A* and *B* are codominant and *O* is recessive. If a man with type O blood mates with a woman with type A blood, the expected proportion of *heterozygotes* among their offspring is _____ depending on the genotype of the woman.
    a. 0 or 25 percent
    b. 25 or 50 percent
    *c. 50 or 100 percent
    d. 75 or 100 percent

32. The *ABO* blood group has three alleles (*A, B, O*) where *A* and *B* are codominant and *O* is recessive. How can a woman with type A blood and a man with type B blood have a child with type O blood?
    a. The woman must have genotype *AA* and the man must have genotype *BO*.
    b. The woman must have genotype *AO* and the man must have genotype *BB*.
    *c. The woman must have genotype *AO* and the man must have genotype *BO*.
    d. These parents can never have a type O child.

13

33. The *MN* blood group has two codominant alleles. How can a woman with type M blood have a child with type N blood?
    a. The father had to have type M blood.
    b. The father had to have type MN blood.
    c. The father had to have type N blood.
    *d. The woman could never have a child with type N blood.

34. The *ABO* blood group has three alleles (*A, B, O*) where *A* and *B* are codominant and *O* is recessive. How can a woman with type O blood have a child with type A blood?
    a. The father has to have genotype *AA* or genotype *AO*.
    b. The father has to have genotype *AA* or genotype *AB*.
    c. The father has to have genotype *AO* or genotype *AB*.
    *d. The father has to have genotype *AA*, genotype *AO*, or genotype *AB*.

35. Mendel's Law of Independent Assortment states that
    a. only one chromosome of each pair is passed on from a parent to an offspring.
    b. sections of the genetic code can cross over from one of a chromosome pair to the other during the production of sex cells.
    c. one allele may be dominant over another.
    *d. the set of chromosomes that is passed on from a parent to a child is not always the same.

36. Imagine an organism with three chromosomes. According to Mendel's Law of Independent Assortment, how many genetically different sex cells could this organism produce?
    a. 1
    *b. 8
    c. 300
    d. 100,000

37. Sometimes alleles for different genes are inherited together, which is due to
    *a. linkage.
    b. crossing-over.
    c. polygenic inheritance.
    d. pleiotropic inheritance.

38. For the human sex chromosomes, males have
    a. two X chromosomes.
    b. two Y chromosomes.
    *c. an X chromosome and a Y chromosome.
    d. only one chromosome—an X.

39. Hemophilia is caused by a recessive allele found on the X chromosome. As such, hemophilia will be
    *a. more common in men than women.
    b. more common in women than men.
    c. equally common in men and women.
    d. rare in women, but never found in men.

40. Traits that are due, in part, to multiple loci are known as _____ traits.
    a. pleiotropic
    b. dominant
    c. polymorphic
    *d. polygenic

41. Some genes can have multiple effects on an organism, such as affecting different physical and biochemical systems. This is known as
    a. polygenic inheritance.
    b. linkage.
    *c. pleiotropy.
    d. crossing-over.

42. Mutations
    a. are always harmful to the individual but may be advantageous for the entire population.
    b. are not random in occurrence; they occur more often where needed.
    c. occur only in small, isolated human populations in the modern world.
    *d. must occur in sex cells to have an evolutionary impact.

43. Mutations are
    a. always harmful.
    b. always neutral.
    c. sometimes harmful, sometimes useful, but never neutral.
    *d. sometimes harmful, sometimes useful, and sometimes neutral.

44. Mutations can involve
    a. deletion of a section of genetic code.
    b. addition of a section of genetic code.
    c. duplication of a section of genetic code.
    *d. All of the above.

45. Conditions such as Down syndrome involve
    a. rearrangement of sections of a chromosome.
    b. deletion of a chromosome, resulting in one chromosome.
    *c. duplication of a chromosome, resulting in three chromosomes.
    d. tripling of a chromosome, resulting in four chromosomes.

46. Sickle cell anemia is due to a mutation that
    *a. changes one base in the genetic code.
    b. duplicates a large section of genetic code.
    c. deletes a large section of genetic code.
    d. duplicates a chromosome.

47. Mutation rates for changes in single bases typically range from
    _____ per million sex cells.
    *a. 1 to 100
    b. 1,000 to 10,000
    c. 100,000 to 500,000
    d. Mutation never occurs.

Essay Questions

48. The simple model of "one locus-one effect" is useful for learning basic genetic principles but is less useful in understanding complex traits. Describe briefly other types of interactions.

49. Assume a person has a single fatal mutation inherited from one of his/her parents. Under what conditions will that person survive, and why?

CHAPTER 3

EVOLUTIONARY THEORY

Overview

This chapter is concerned with the process of evolution as viewed from two perspectives—microevolution (changes in allele frequency over short periods of time) and macroevolution (long-term evolutionary change, including the origin of new species). The first part of the chapter provides some basic background in population genetics, starting with consideration of Hardy-Weinberg equilibrium and proceeding with a discussion of the four evolutionary forces (mutation, selection, genetic drift, gene flow). The second part of the chapter examines the origin of species and several patterns in macroevolution. The chapter concludes with a discussion of some common misconceptions regarding evolution.

Outline

I. Microevolution
   A. Population Genetics
      1. Genotype and allele frequencies
      2. Hardy-Weinberg equilibrium
   B. Evolutionary Forces
      1. Mutation
      2. Natural selection
      3. Genetic drift
      4. Gene flow
      5. Interaction of the evolutionary forces

II. Macroevolution
   A. Taxonomy and Evolution
      1. Taxonomic categories
      2. The biological species concept
      3. Modes of species change
   B. Patterns of Macroevolution
      1. Speciation
      2. Adaptive radiation
      3. The tempo and mode of macroevolution
      4. Extinctions and mass extinctions

III. Misconceptions About Evolution
    A. The Nature of Selection
        1. Misconception: bigger is better
        2. Misconception: newer is better
        3. Misconception: natural selection always works
        4. Misconception: there is an inevitable direction in evolution
    B. Structure, Function, and Evolution
        1. Misconception: natural selection always produces perfect structures
        2. Misconception: all structures are adaptive
        3. Misconception: current structures always reflect initial adaptations

IV. Summary

V. Supplemental Readings

    Special Topic: Science Fiction and Orthogenesis

Topics for Discussion

1. Perform some simple microevolutionary experiments to demonstrate the evolutionary forces. Computer demonstrations, given available equipment, are very useful in this context (a simple program is available from the author). If computers are not available, microevolutionary "experiments" can be performed using random numbers, colored beads, or other material.

2. With the use of the formulae presented in Appendix 1, assign students different parameters for selection, gene flow, and so on, and compare the results in class.

3. Suggest hypothetical examples of allele frequency change and ask what evolutionary force(s) might be most responsible for the observed change.

4. Use additional examples to discuss problems in classification of fossils. For example, *Archaeopteryx*—was it a bird or a reptile?

5. Discuss the importance of chance in evolutionary history, and contrast it with earlier views on predestined paths in evolution.

6. Show a clip from a science fiction show or movie that deals with some issue of evolution (the future of human evolution is a common theme). Point out examples of misconceptions about evolution.

Multiple-Choice Questions

Correct answers are marked with an asterisk (*). There are multiple questions for certain topics.

1. The definition of a "breeding population" can be influenced by
   a. geographic distribution.
   b. cultural differences.
   c. the age distribution of the population.
   *d. All of the above.

2. In terms of the *MN* blood group, consider a population that has 50 people with genotype *MM*, 100 people with genotype *MN*, and 50 people with genotype *NN*. What are the *genotype frequencies* of this population?
   *a. *MM* = 0.25, *MN* = 0.50, *NN* = 0.25
   b. *MM* = 0.50, *MN* = 1.00, *NN* = 0.50
   c. *MM* = 0.50, *MN* = 0.50, *NN* = 0.00
   d. *MM* = 0.00, *MN* = 0.50, *NN* = 0.50

3. There are three phenotypes for the *MN* blood group: M, MN, and M. Consider a population with 72 people with blood type M, 96 people with blood type MN, and 32 people with blood type N. What is the proportion of people with blood type MN in this population?
   a. 0.40
   b. 0.60
   *c. 0.48
   d. 0.96

4. The PTC-tasting locus has two alleles, *T* and *t*, where *T* is dominant and is the "tasting" allele. If the *genotype* frequencies are *TT* = 0.49, *Tt* =.42, and *tt* = 0.09, what proportion of this population are tasters?
   a. 0.98
   *b. 0.91
   c. 0.49
   d. 0.42

5. In terms of the *MN* blood group, assume a population that has 49 people with genotype *MM*, 42 people with genotype *MN*, and 9 people with genotype *NN*. What is the frequency of the *M* allele in this population?
   a. 0.30
   b. 0.42
   c. 0.49
   *d. 0.70

6. Imagine a locus with two alleles, A and a. If there are 4 people with genotype AA, 32 people with genotype Aa, and 64 people with genotype aa, what is the frequency of the A allele?
   *a. 0.20
   b. 0.32
   c. 0.64
   d. 0.80

7. Imagine a locus with two alleles, A and a. If there are 72 people with genotype AA, 96 people with genotype Aa, and 32 people with genotype aa, what is the frequency of the A allele?
   a. 0.32
   *b. 0.60
   c. 0.72
   d. 1.00

8. Imagine a locus with two alleles, A and a. If there are 81 people with genotype AA, 18 people with genotype Aa, and 1 person with genotype aa, what is the frequency of the A allele?
   a. 0.18
   b. 0.81
   *c. 0.90
   d. 1.00

9. Imagine a locus with two alleles, A and a. If there are 50 A alleles and 150 a alleles in the population, what is the frequency of the A allele?
   a. 0.15
   b. 0.33
   c. 0.50
   *d. 0.75

10. In terms of the MN blood group, assume a population that has 25 people with genotype MM, 50 people with genotype MN, and 25 people with genotype NN. How many M alleles are in the population?
   a. 25
   b. 50
   *c. 100
   d. 200

11. In terms of the *MN* blood group, assume a population that has 31 people with genotype *MM*, 54 people with genotype *MN*, and 22 people with genotype *NN*. How many total alleles are in the population?
   a. 31
   b. 54
   c. 107
   *d. 214

12. Imagine a locus with two alleles, *F* and *G*. If the frequency of the *F* allele is 0.6, then the frequency of the *G* allele must be
   a. 0.0.
   *b. 0.4.
   c. 0.6.
   d. 1.0.

13. Hardy-Weinberg equilibrium states that
   *a. under certain conditions, allele frequencies will remain constant over time.
   b. the less common allele will eventually disappear.
   c. if an allele is recessive, it will eventually disappear.
   d. evolution often consists of very rapid changes over a single generation.

14. Imagine an allele frequency of 0.7 in a given population. If this population meets the assumption of Hardy-Weinberg equilibrium, the allele frequency will _____ in the next generation.
   a. decrease
   b. increase
   *c. stay the same
   d. This question cannot be answered given the available data.

15. You visit a random mating population and find that the observed genotype frequencies are *not* what would be expected under Hardy-Weinberg equilibrium. What does this tell you?
   a. Hardy and Weinberg were wrong.
   b. Your data must be contaminated.
   *c. Evolution has occurred.
   d. Evolution has not occurred.

16. Assume two alleles, *A* and *B*, at a given locus. If the frequency of the *A* allele is 0.6 and the frequency of the *a* allele is 0.4, the expected genotype frequencies are:
   a. $AA = 0.16$, $Aa = 0.42$, $aa = 0.36$
   b. $AA = 0.60$, $Aa = 0.00$, $aa = 0.40$
   *c. $AA = 0.36$, $Aa = 0.42$, $aa = 0.16$
   d. $AA = 1.00$, $Aa = 0.00$, $aa = 0.00$

17. Assume two alleles, *A* and *B*, at a given locus. If the frequency of
the *A* allele is 0.2 and the frequency of the *a* allele is 0.8, the
expected genotype frequencies are:
    a. *AA* = 0.16, *Aa* = 0.00, *aa* = 0.84
    b. *AA* = 0.20, *Aa* = 0.00, *aa* = 0.80
    c. *AA* = 0.64, *Aa* = 0.32, *aa* = 0.04
    *d. *AA* = 0.04, *Aa* = 0.32, *aa* = 0.64

18. Assume two alleles, *A* and *B*, at a given locus. If the frequency of
the *A* allele is 0.3 and the frequency of the *B* allele is 0.7, then
what is the expected frequency of genotype *AA*?
    *a. 0.09
    b. 0.30
    c. 0.49
    d. 0.70

19. Assume two alleles, *A* and *B*, at a given locus. If the frequency of
the *A* allele is 0.8 and the frequency of the *B* allele is 0.2, then
what is the expected frequency of genotype *AB*?
    a. 0.16
    b. 0.20
    *c. 0.32
    d. 0.80

20. Assume two alleles, *A* and *B*, at a given locus. If the frequency of
the *A* allele is 0.7, what is the expected frequency of the genotype
BB?
    *a. 0.09
    b. 0.21
    c. 0.30
    d. 0.42

21. Assume a locus where there is an occasional mutation from the *A*
allele to the *B* allele. Under these circumstances, the frequency of
the *B* allele will
    a. completely replace the *A* allele in a single generation.
    b. decrease over time.
    c. stay the same.
    *d. increase over time.

22. Assume the frequency of an allele has changed from 0.30 to 0.58 in a single generation in the population you are studying. This change is not likely to have been caused by mutation. Why?
   a. Mutations do not occur anymore.
   *b. Mutations occur less often than this.
   c. Mutations generally cause allele frequencies to attain values of 0.0 or 1.0 in a single generation.
   d. Mutation is the only way in which allele frequencies can change.

23. The probability of survival and reproduction of an organism is known as its
   a. genotype.
   b. phenotype.
   *c. fitness.
   d. mutation rate.

24. Fitness refers to an organism's
   *a. probability of survival and reproduction.
   b. physical fitness.
   c. age.
   d. body shape.

25. Imagine a locus with two alleles, A and Z, where individuals with the genotype AA are more resistant to a given disease than those with genotypes AZ or ZZ. This is an example of
   a. genetic drift.
   b. gene flow.
   *c. natural selection.
   d. mutation.

26. Imagine a locus with two alleles, A and Z, where individuals with the genotype AZ generally have more offspring than those with genotypes AA or ZZ. This is an example of
   a. mutation.
   b. gene flow.
   c. genetic drift.
   *d. natural selection.

27. Selection against a recessive allele will
   a. completely remove the allele in a single generation.
   b. will gradually increase the frequency of the recessive allele.
   *c. will gradually decrease the frequency of the recessive allele.
   d. will result in a balance where both allele frequencies are equal to 0.5.

28. *Complete* selection against a recessive allele will not remove that allele in a single generation. Why?
    *a. The heterozygotes in the population will continue to carry the allele.
    b. There is no such thing as complete selection against an allele.
    c. Actually, this will occur as long as the initial frequency of the recessive allele is less than 0.5.
    d. Genetic drift will remove the allele before selection can occur.

29. Natural selection often removes one allele and increases the frequency of another allele. _____, however, can result in a *balance* of allele frequencies without removing any alleles from the population.
    *a. Selection *for* the heterozygote
    b. Selection *against* a recessive allele
    c. Selection *against* a dominant allele
    d. Selection *against* the heterozygote

30. Suppose you have been observing natural selection in a population and note that the frequency of an allele has increased to 0.7, but doesn't change after this level is reached. What kind of selection is responsible?
    a. Selection *against* a recessive allele.
    b. Selection *for* a recessive allele.
    c. Selection *against* the heterozygote.
    *d. Selection *for* the heterozygote.

31. Which of the following is a characteristic of genetic drift?
    a. The larger the population, the greater its effect.
    *b. The smaller the population, the greater its effect.
    c. Population size has no effect on the extent of genetic drift.
    d. It never occurs in human populations.

32. Given enough time, genetic drift will eventually cause
    *a. the loss of alleles.
    b. an increase in genetic variation within a population.
    c. an increase in the mutation rate.
    d. extinction of the species.

33. The genetics of the Dunker population in the United States suggests that _____ was the primary factor causing allele frequency changes, due to their relatively small population size.
    a. mutation
    b. natural selection
    c. gene flow
    *d. genetic drift

34. Gene flow acts to make populations
   *a.   more similar to each other.
    b.   less similar to each other.
    c.   completely different from one another in a single generation.
    d.   None of the above.

35. _____ can reduce gene flow between human populations.
    a.   Geographic distance
    b.   Language differences
    c.   Social differences
   *d.   All of the above.

36. Genetic *differences* between populations can be caused by
    a.   gene flow and genetic drift.
   *b.   genetic drift and natural selection.
    c.   gene flow and natural selection.
    d.   gene flow, genetic drift, and natural selection.

37. If a *very large* population is *totally isolated* and the frequency of an
    allele changes from 0.45 to 0.30 in a single generation, this
    change is most likely due to
   *a.   natural selection.
    b.   genetic drift.
    c.   mutation.
    d.   gene flow.

38. New alleles can be brought into a population by
    a.   mutation and genetic drift.
    b.   mutation and natural selection.
   *c.   mutation and gene flow.
    d.   gene flow and natural selection.

39. You observe a change in allele frequency in a population from
    0.1 to 0.4 in a single generation. The population is small (25
    people) and exchanges many mates with surrounding
    populations. This change could be due to
    a.   mutation.
   *b.   gene flow and/or genetic drift.
    c.   gene flow, but not genetic drift.
    d.   genetic drift, but not gene flow.

40. Imagine you see the frequency of a harmful allele *increase*
    slightly over time in an isolated population. What could be
    responsible for this contradictory observation?
    a.   gene flow
    b.   inbreeding
   *c.   genetic drift
    d.   This could never happen.

41. Genetic drift acts to _____ variation within populations and _____ variation between populations.
    a. decrease / decrease
    b. increase / increase
    *c. decrease / increase
    d. increase / decrease

42. Gene flow acts to _____ variation within populations and _____ variation between populations.
    a. decrease / decrease
    *b. increase / increase
    c. decrease / increase
    d. increase / decrease

43. Natural selection can act to _____ variation between populations.
    a. increase
    b. decrease
    *c. increase or decrease
    d. None of the above.

44. According to the biological species concept, horses and donkeys are *not* considered in the same species because
    a. they never mate.
    *b. they do not produce fertile offspring.
    c. they look different.
    d. they do not share a relatively recent common ancestor.

45. The transformation of a species over time is known as
    a. polygenesis.
    b. monogenesis.
    c. cladogenesis.
    *d. anagenesis.

46. The origin of a new species *first* requires
    *a. reduced gene flow.
    b. increased gene flow.
    c. reduced mutation rates.
    d. increased mutation rates.

47. Someone comes up to you and states that an early species of ape could not have evolved into the first humans because both apes and humans are alive today. This person has failed to grasp the nature of
    a. polygenesis.
    b. monogenesis.
    *c. cladogenesis.
    d. anagenesis.

48. _____ is when a species gives rise to a new and separate species.
    a. Polygenesis
    b. Monogenesis
    *c. Cladogenesis
    d. Anagenesis

49. _____ acts to inhibit reproductive isolation.
    a. Mutation
    b. Natural selection
    c. Genetic drift
    *d. Gene flow

50. When we place fossil specimens into different species based on their physical appearance, we are using the _____ concept.
    a. biological species
    *b. paleospecies
    c. anagenetic species
    d. monospecies

51. Rapid speciation following the availability of new environments is known as
    a. gradualism.
    b. punctuated equilibrium.
    c. species selection.
    *d. adaptive radiation.

52. In your study of the fossil record of early mammals, you notice a changing environment is followed by the initial appearance of a tree-climbing species, which is then followed by many later tree-climbing species. This is an example of
    a. anagenesis.
    b. gradualism.
    c. species selection.
    *d. adaptive radiation.

53. According to the idea of gradualism, macroevolution usually involves
    *a. slow and gradual change.
    b. most species becoming extinct in a relatively short time.
    c. alternating periods of stasis (no change) and rapid change.
    d. species selection.

54. According to the idea of punctuated equilibrium, macroevolution usually involves
    a. slow and gradual change.
    b. most species becoming extinct in a relatively short time.
    *c. alternating periods of stasis (no change) and rapid change.
    d. species selection.

55. The pattern of evolutionary change shown on the board is
    a. gradualism (linear).
    b. gradualism (geometric).
    *c. punctuated equilibrium.
    d. species selection.

Note: The instructor must draw a picture (or show a slide) of punctuated equilibrium.

56. The pattern of evolutionary change shown on the board is
    *a. gradualism (linear).
    b. gradualism (geometric).
    c. punctuated equilibrium.
    d. species selection.

Note: The instructor must draw a picture (or show a slide) of gradualism (linear).

57. How common has extinction been in the fossil record?
    *a. Over 99 percent of all past species have become extinct.
    b. Roughly 50 percent of all past species have become extinct.
    c. Roughly 25 percent of all past species have become extinct.
    d. Very few species have ever become extinct.

58. A mass extinction is
    a. the extinction of small-sized species.
    b. the extinction of large-sized species.
    *c. the simultaneous extinction of many species.
    d. something that has never been seen in the fossil record.

59. The idea that evolution will continue in the same direction is known as orthogenesis. This idea
    *a. is incorrect—not all structures continue to change in the same direction.
    b. is always correct.
    c. is correct for all organisms except for humans.
    d. is also known as natural selection.

60. The idea that natural selection will always select for larger organisms ("bigger is better")
    a. is totally supported by both the fossil evidence and field studies of living species.
    b. fails to consider the fact that smaller individuals often have an advantage in terms of disease resistance.
    *c. fails to consider the fact that smaller individuals often require less food and are therefore sometimes at an advantage.
    d. is true for mammals and reptiles, but seldom for other groups of animals.

61. The more recent a trait has evolved
    a. the "better" it is in an evolutionary sense.
    b. the more quickly a species will become extinct.
    c. the more likely the effect of genetic drift.
    *d. has no bearing on its worth compared with other traits that are older.

62. Natural selection
    a. always works.
    b. always produces perfect structures.
    c. always leads to an increase in size.
    *d. None of the above.

Essay Questions

63. Assume you are studying the genetics of a locus with a lethal recessive allele that has increased in frequency from one generation to the next in an isolated population. Describe two ways in which this scenario could occur.

64. Assume you have visited a population of 500 people and have found the following genotype numbers for the MN blood group system: MM = 24, MN = 152, NN = 324. What are the allele frequencies? Does the population seem to be in Hardy-Weinberg equilibrium? If not, what factors are most likely responsible for the difference between observed and expected genotype numbers?

65. What type of evolutionary pattern can be inferred from the attached graph? Gradualism? Punctuated equilibrium? Both? Neither? Why? (Note to instructor: provide a challenging example, such as a graph of hominid brain size versus time.)

66. What are the possible dangers in assigning different species names to specimens that differ in size?

67. Examine some popular image (from film, TV, magazines, etc.) that you are familiar with and describe any evolutionary misconceptions that are apparent (e.g., *King Kong*, certain episodes of *Star Trek*, and so on).

CHAPTER 4

THE PRIMATES

Overview

This chapter focuses on general issues of mammalian and primate taxonomy. The chapter begins with a brief introduction to methods of classification. Following this introduction, the chapter first considers humans as animals, chordates, vertebrates, and mammals. The chapter then moves on to consider primate characteristics. The final part of the chapter examines different approaches to the analysis of primate behavior (socioecology and sociobiology).

Outline

I. Taxonomy
   A. Methods of Classification
      1. Homologous and analogous traits
      2. Primitive and derived traits
   B. The Vertebrates
      1. The animal kingdom
      2. Vertebrate characteristics

II. The Mammals
   A. Reproduction
      1. Placental mammals
      2. Parental care
   B. Temperature Regulation
   C. Teeth
   D. Skeletal Structure
   E. Behavior

III. Primate Characteristics
   A. The Skeleton
      1. Grasping hands
      2. Generalized structure
   B. Vision
   C. The Brain and Behavior
   D. Reproduction and Care of Offspring
      1. The mother-infant bond
      2. Paternal care
      3. Growing up

    E.   Social Structure
        1. Social groups
        2. Social organization and dominance

IV.   Types of Primates
    A. Prosimians
    B. Anthropoids

V.   The Monkeys
    A. New World Monkeys
    B. Old World Monkeys

VI.   The Living Apes
    A. The Hominoids
    B. Gibbons and Siamangs
    C. Orangutans
    D. Gorillas
    E. Chimpanzees
    F. Bonobos

VII.   Summary

VIII. Supplemental Readings

Special Topic: Social Structure and Testes Size in Primates

Topics for Discussion

1. Ask students for comparison of humans with several nonprimate mammals. Focus on similarities and differences in both biology and behavior.

2. Given the difference between modern mammals and modern reptiles, how can we discuss the evolution of mammals from reptiles. Discuss and critique the "missing link" concept. Discuss the nature of evolutionary transitions.

3. What other types of mammals have adapted, at least partially, to life in the trees? Use this as a springboard for discussing multiple "solutions" in evolution.

4. Discuss whether variation in primate social structure reflects genetic factors, environmental factors, or both. How can these ideas be tested?

5. Show selected scenes from a film on primate behavior, but with the sound turned off so that students cannot hear the narration. Ask for and discuss interpretations of the observed behaviors.

6. Discuss controversies regarding the use of the terms "ape" and "human." Should humans be classified with the African apes to the exclusion of the orangutan? What are the implications of this classification?

7. Why isn't it a simple matter to define the social structure and organization of "apes"?

8. Humans have often been called "naked apes." Is this accurate?

Multiple-Choice Questions

Correct answers are marked with an asterisk (*). There are multiple questions for certain topics.

1. The limbs of humans and many other vertebrates consist of an upper limb bone and two lower limb bones. This similarity among many vertebrates is an example of a _____ trait.
   a. polygenic
   b. nonadaptive
   c. analogous
   *d. homologous

2. Which of the following pairs are analogous traits?
   a. Number of teeth in humans / Number of teeth in apes
   b. Upright walking in humans / Large brain size in humans
   c. Number of limbs in cats / Number of limbs in dogs
   *d. Bird's wing / Insect's wing

3. An example of a primitive trait in modern humans is
   *a. five digits on hands and feet.
   b. a large brain.
   c. small canine teeth.
   d. tool use.

4. An example of a derived trait in humans (compared to apes) is
   a. forward facing eyes.
   b. five digits on hands and feet.
   c. the number of molar teeth.
   *d. upright walking.

5. A _____ trait is one that has been inherited from an earlier ancestor.
   a. analogous
   b. homologous
   c. derived
   *d. primitive

6. A _____ trait is one that has changed from an ancestral state.
   a. homologous
   b. analogous
   c. primitive
   *d. derived

7. Neither apes nor humans have a tail, whereas other primates have tails. Compared with apes, the lack of a tail in human beings is a _____ trait since they both inherited it from a common ancestor.
   a. analogous
   b. homologous
   *c. primitive
   d. derived

8. All living organisms can be placed into one of _____ kingdoms.
   *a. 5
   b. 4
   c. 3
   d. 2

9. Humans belong in the _____ kingdom.
   a. vertebrate
   b. primate
   c. mammalian
   *d. animal

10. The chordates are animals with
    a. teeth.
    b. five fingers and toes.
    *c. a spinal cord.
    d. mammary glands.

11. Which of the following is *not* a characteristic of vertebrates?
    a. Bilateral symmetry.
    *b. They all have teeth.
    c. An internal spinal cord.
    d. A backbone.

12. Compared to modern reptiles, modern mammals have _____ offspring with _____ parental care.
    a. fewer / less
    *b. fewer / more
    c. more / less
    d. more/ more

13. How do mammals (the entire group) reproduce?
    a. All have live births.
    b. All lay eggs.
    *c. Some lay eggs, and others have live births.
    d. None of the above.

14. The placenta functions to
    a. provide food to the fetus.
    b. provide oxygen to the fetus.
    c. filter out waste products.
    *d. All of the above.

15. Mammary glands are found in _____ and provide _____ to newborns.
    *a. mammals / food
    b. mammals / oxygen
    c. reptiles / food
    d. reptiles / oxygen

16. Modern _____ are able to maintain a constant body temperature.
    a. fish
    b. reptiles
    *c. mammals
    d. All of the above.

17. How does the pattern of reproduction and child care in humans differ from other mammals?
    *a. Humans have more offspring without sacrificing care.
    b. Humans have fewer offspring.
    c. Humans have more offspring, but sacrifice care.
    d. There is no difference.

18. There are _____ different types of mammalian teeth.
    a. 1
    b. 2
    c. 3
    *d. 4

19. The _____ teeth are used for chewing.
    a. canine and molar
    *b. premolar and molar
    c. premolar and incisor
    d. incisor and canine

20. Imagine you are looking at a jaw with incisors, canines, premolars, and molars. This jaw belongs to a modern
    a. fish.
    b. reptile.
    *c. mammal.
    d. bird.

21. Humans are different from most other mammals in having _____ canine teeth.
    a. larger
    *b. smaller
    c. more
    d. fewer

22. The _____ is the part of the brain associated with learning, memory, and intelligence.
    a. pineal gland
    *b. cerebrum
    c. hypothalamus
    d. occipital lobe

23. One of the characteristics of primates is
    a. claws instead of nails.
    b. specialized limb structure compared to other vertebrates.
    *c. binocular stereoscopic vision.
    d. an emphasis on smell rather than vision.

24. Grasping hands and depth perception are important in coping with _____ environment.
    *a. an arboreal
    b. a terrestrial
    c. an aquatic
    d. a desert

25. Primate hands are different from those of other mammals—primates have
    a. claws instead of nails.
    *b. nails instead of claws.
    c. more fingers on average.
    d. fewer fingers on average.

26. Primates have _____ vision.
    a. black and white
    *b. binocular stereoscopic
    c. microscopic
    d. very limited

27. Compared to most other mammals, primates rely more on
    a. smell than sight.
    *b. sight than smell.
    c. touch than sight.
    d. hearing than sight.

28. Which of the following bonds is strongest in primate societies?
    a. sexual
    b. between adult males
    c. sibling
    *d. mother-infant

29. Paternal care is most common in _____ primate societies.
    a. polygamous
    *b. monogamous
    c. very large
    d. meat-eating

30. The most common type of social group found in primate
    societies is the _____ group.
    a. uni-male
    *b. multimale/multifemale
    c. family
    d. solitary

31. A _____ group consists of a single adult male, several
    adult females, and their offspring.
    a. multimale/multifemale
    *b. uni-male
    c. family
    d. solitary

32. The ranking system within a primate society is known as the
    a. gender hierarchy.
    b. differential status ladder.
    *c. dominance hierarchy.
    d. class structure.

33. An individual's place in the dominance hierarchy of many primate societies can be determined by
    a. strength and physical ability.
    b. dominance rank of his mother.
    c. age.
    *d. All of the above.

34. The _____ are the most biologically primitive of modern primates.
    *a. prosimians
    b. hominoids
    c. New World monkeys
    d. Old World monkeys

35. Which of the following is *not* a characteristic of prosimians?
    a. Many have a single claw on each hand.
    *b. They all live in multimale/multifemale groups.
    c. They tend to rely more on a sense of smell than other primates.
    d. Some are nocturnal.

36. Which of the following is *not* a prosimian?
    a. lemur
    *b. monkey
    c. loris
    d. tarsier

37. The primate group known as anthropoids consists of
    a. prosimians and apes.
    b. Old World monkeys, apes, and humans, but *not* New World monkeys.
    c. New World monkeys, Old World monkeys, and apes, but *not* humans.
    *d. all monkeys, apes, and humans.

38. Anthropoids live in
    a. Africa.
    b. Asia.
    c. the New World.
    *d. All of the above.

39. Unlike other prosimians, tarsiers
    *a. do not have a moist nose.
    b. live in the trees.
    c. are nocturnal.
    d. live in Asia.

40. Monkeys are found in
    a. the New World, but not the Old World.
    b. the Old World, but not the New World.
    *c. both the New World and Old World.
    d. Africa only.

41. New World monkeys have _____ teeth than Old World monkeys.
    a. fewer premolar
    *b. more premolar
    c. fewer canine
    d. more canine

42. You go to the zoo and spot a primate hanging by its tail. What is it?
    a. a prosimian
    *b. a New World monkey
    c. an Old World monkey
    d. an ape

43. New World monkeys are
    *a. arboreal.
    b. terrestrial.
    c. arboreal and terrestrial.
    d. nocturnal.

44. Which of the following is most similar biologically to human beings?
    a. lemurs
    b. tarsiers
    c. New World monkeys
    *d. Old World monkeys

45. _____ have front and rear limbs of equal size, with their spines parallel to the ground when they walk on all fours.
    *a. Monkeys
    b. Asian apes
    c. African apes
    d. All apes

46. Hominoids differ from monkeys in that hominoids
    *a. are capable of suspensory hanging (arms above their head).
    b. have fewer teeth than all other anthropoids.
    c. are the only primate capable of passing on learned behavior to offspring.
    d. have a tail.

47. Hominoids consist of
    a. monkeys and apes.
    *b. apes and humans
    c. prosimians and monkeys.
    d. monkeys, apes, and humans.

48. How are the teeth of apes and humans different?
    a. different number of incisors
    b. different number of premolars
    c. different number of molars
    *d. None of the above

49. Which group of primates would be most at home swinging by
    their arms at the "monkey bars" found in most playgrounds?
    a. tarsiers
    b. lemurs and lorises
    *c. hominoids
    d. monkeys

50. Which primate has longer arms than legs?
    *a. apes
    b. monkeys
    c. humans
    d. prosimians

51. The living apes are found in
    a. Africa.
    b. Asia.
    *c. Africa and Asia.
    d. Africa, Asia, and Europe.

52. The African apes consist of
    a. chimpanzees, gorillas, and baboons.
    b. chimpanzees, gorillas, and gibbons.
    c. gorillas, bonobos, and gibbons.
    *d. chimpanzees, gorillas, and bonobos.

53. The Asian apes consist of
    a. the gorilla and the orangutan.
    b. the gibbon (including the siamang) and the gorilla.
    *c. the gibbon (including the siamang) and the orangutan.
    d. the chimpanzee and the orangutan.

54. African apes are genetically (and evolutionarily) the most similar to
   *a. humans.
   b. orangutans.
   c. Old World monkeys.
   d. New World monkeys.

55. The DNA sequences of humans and chimpanzees are
   a. totally different.
   b. roughly 80 to 90 percent identical.
   *c. over 98 percent identical.
   d. are not known in sufficient detail to make any statements regarding similarity.

56. Gibbons (and siamangs) are
   a. vertical clingers and leapers.
   b. knuckle walkers.
   *c. arm-swingers.
   d. bipeds.

57. What type of social group is found in gibbons?
   a. solitary
   *b. family
   c. uni-male
   d. multimale/multifemale

58. How different is the adult body size of male and female orangutans?
   *a. Males are roughly twice the size of females.
   b. Males are slightly larger than females.
   c. They are about the same size.
   d. Females are slightly larger than males.

59. In the trees, orangutans are
   *a. climbers and hangers.
   b. knuckle walkers.
   c. vertical clingers and leapers.
   d. bipeds.

60. Orangutans are found in
   a. Africa.
   *b. Asia.
   c. Europe.
   d. Africa and Asia.

61. What type of social group is found in orangutans?
   *a. solitary
   b. family
   c. uni-male
   d. multimale/multifemale

62. How do large adult male orangutans get from one tree to another?
   *a. They rock the trees back and forth till they bend near one another.
   b. They jump through the air.
   c. They swing on vines.
   d. They are carried by smaller, less dominant males.

63. _____ are knuckle walkers.
   a. Old World monkeys.
   b. New World monkeys.
   *c. African apes.
   d. Asian apes.

64. Gorilla groups have one _____, known as the silverback.
   a. adult female
   *b. adult male
   c. infant (male or female)
   d. teenager (male or female)

65. Gorillas are found in
   *a. forests in Africa.
   b. forests in Asia.
   c. the African savanna.
   d. the mountains of Asia.

66. What type of social group is found in gorillas?
   a. solitary
   b. family
   *c. uni-male
   d. multimale/multifemale

67. Chimpanzees are
   a. vertical clingers and leapers.
   b. climbers and hangers.
   *c. knuckle walkers.
   d. bipeds.

68. What is the difference in adult body size of male and female chimpanzees?
    a. Females are slightly larger than males.
    b. Females are twice the size of males.
    *c. Males are slightly larger than females.
    d. Males are twice the size of females.

69. What type of social group is found in chimpanzees?
    a. solitary
    b. family
    c. uni-male
    *d. multimale/multifemale

70. A chimpanzee will tend to associate with its _____, even after it is fully grown.
    *a. mother
    b. father
    c. sister(s)
    d. brother(s)

71. Even though it is about the same size, the _____ has been referred to as a "pygmy chimpanzee."
    a. gibbon
    b. baboon
    c. gorilla
    *d. bonobo

72. In bonobo society, _____ tend to be the most dominant.
    a. adult males
    *b. adult females
    c. teenage males
    d. Adult males and females are equally dominant.

73. How do bonobos reduce tension (in a manner different from other primates)?
    a. grooming
    *b. sex play
    c. aggressive behavior
    d. eating

74. What type of social group is found in bonobos?
    a. solitary
    b. family
    c. uni-male
    *d. multimale/multifemale

75. Primate species with the _____ type of social group tend to have larger testes than expected from their body size.
    a. solitary
    b. family
    c. uni-male
    *d. multimale/multifemale

Essay Questions

76. Why do mammals have different types of teeth? How does this characteristic relate to other mammalian characteristics?

77. If culture is defined simply as learned behavior, then can we say that nonhuman primates have culture? Use data from the Japanese macaque study to defend your answer.

78. Cartoons frequently portray nonhuman animals as all living in "families" similar to Western society. Why is this portrayal inaccurate?

79. Describe some aspect of primate behavior that shows the influence of the physical environment (e.g., food resource distribution, presence or absence of predators, and so on).

80. Describe the similarities and differences of the prosimian/anthropoid and strepsirhine/haplorhine classification systems.

81. Human children frequently play on the "monkey bars" at playgrounds. Why is this term inaccurate? Be specific.

82. Suppose someone has made the claim to you that social structure of primates is completely genetically determined, and that, therefore, related groups of primates should have the same social structure. Reject this argument using data from the living apes.

CHAPTER 5

THE HUMAN SPECIES

Overview

This chapter focuses on the human species in taxonomic and evolutionary perspective. The first part of the chapter looks at unique human characteristics, including large brain size, bipedalism, and small canines. The human life cycle is also examined, including patterns of reproduction and physical growth. The second part of the chapter examines two areas once thought to be uniquely human—tool making and language acquisition.

Outline

I.   Characteristics of Living Humans
     A. Distribution and Environment
     B. Brain Size and Structure
     C. Bipedalism
     D. Canine Teeth
     E. Sex and Reproduction
     F. Human Growth
        1. Prenatal growth
        2. The pattern of human postnatal growth
     G. Social Structure

II. Are Humans Unique?
     A. Tool Use and Manufacture
        1. Chimpanzee termite fishing
        2. Other examples of toolmaking
        3. Human and chimpanzee toolmaking
     B. Language Capabilities
        1. What is language?
        2. Apes and American Sign Language
        3. Human and ape language abilities

III. Summary

IV. Supplemental Readings

     Special Topic: Can Apes Make Stone Tools?

Topics for Discussion

1. How does toolmaking differ between apes and humans?

2. How does language acquisition differ between apes and humans?

3. How has the question "what are humans" been discussed in both science and the arts?

Multiple-Choice Questions

Correct answers are marked with an asterisk (*). There are multiple questions for certain topics.

1. The term "hominid" refers to
   a. modern humans only.
   *b. modern humans and their ancestors back to the initial split from African apes.
   c. human ancestors, but not modern humans.
   d. any biped with a modern human brain size.

2. Allometry refers to
   a. gradual change of a species over time.
   b. the different measurement scales used in studying human variation.
   *c. the fact that different parts of an organism grow at different rates.
   d. measurements taken on the dinosaur *Allosaurus*.

3. The brain size of modern humans is ____ times larger than expected based on body size.
   a. 1.5
   b. 2
   *c. 3
   d. 4

4. Roughly ____ percent of the variation in IQ scores is related to variation in *relative* brain size.
   a. 0
   *b. 16
   c. 56
   d. 100

5. The average brain size of adult human males is somewhat larger than the average brain size of adult human females. Claims that this difference indicates that males should be on average smarter than females fail to consider the fact that
   *a. males have larger body sizes.
   b. females have larger body sizes.
   c. males and females are approximately the same body size.
   d. no one has measured intelligence in adult females.

6. Roughly ____ percent of a modern human's metabolic energy is used by the brain.
   a. 0
   b. 5
   *c. 20
   d. 50

7. How is an ape big toe different from a human big toe?
   a. Apes don't have a big toe.
   *b. The ape's big toe is divergent.
   c. Apes have two big toes on each foot.
   d. The ape's big toe is located on the other side of the foot.

8. Viewed from the front, the upper leg bones
   a. slant outwards away from the body.
   *b. are closer together at the knees.
   c. are completely parallel.
   d. are of different lengths.

9. The spinal column of hominids is
   a. parallel to the ground.
   b. is the exact same shape as that of an ape.
   c. is completely straight.
   *d. curved in several places.

10. Compared to an ape pelvis, a human pelvis is
    a. shorter top to bottom, and narrower side to side.
    b. taller top to bottom, and narrower side to side.
    *c. shorter top to bottom, and wider side to side.
    d. taller top to bottom, and wider side to side.

11. Which of the following is *not* a physical characteristic of bipedalism?
    a. a vertically oriented spine that is curved in several places
    b. legs angle in from the hips to the knees (when viewed from the front)
    *c. the big toe sticks out from the other toes
    d. shortening and widening of the pelvis

12. Humans have
    a. more canine teeth than chimpanzees.
    b. fewer canine teeth than chimpanzees.
    c. larger canine teeth than chimpanzees.
    *d. smaller canine teeth than chimpanzees.

13. The picture on the board is a
    *a. velocity curve for human height.
    b. velocity curve for human brain size.
    c. distance curve for human height.
    d. distance curve for human brain size.

Note: The instructor must draw a picture (or show a slide) of a velocity curve for human height.

14. The picture on the board is a
    a. velocity curve for human height.
    b. velocity curve for human brain size.
    c. distance curve for human height.
    *d. distance curve for human brain size.

Note: The instructor must draw a picture (or show a slide) of a distance curve for human brain size.

15. The fastest *rate* of body size growth occurs during
    *a. infancy.
    b. childhood.
    c. adolescence.
    d. adulthood.

16. The human growth pattern for body size differs from that of other primates by having an *increase* in growth velocity during
    a. childhood.
    b. the juvenile stage.
    *c. adolescence.
    d. adulthood.

17. A unique characteristic of human growth is the
    a. high rate of infant growth.
    b. development of sexual maturity by age 7.
    c. increased growth velocity during adulthood.
    *d. extended childhood.

18. Which part of the body reaches adult size the earliest?
    a. height
    b. weight
    c. reproductive organs
    *d. the head and brain

19. Polyandry is a marriage system where
    a. a man has several wives.
    *b. a woman has several husbands.
    c. several men and several women are all intermarried ("group marriage").
    d. each woman has one husband.

20. In her cross-cultural analysis, Helen Fisher notes that *for all practical purposes,* _____ is the predominant marriage pattern.
    a. polygyny
    b. polyandry
    *c. monogamy
    d. group marriage

21. Examples of tool use among chimpanzees include
    a. "fishing" for termites and ants.
    b. using chewed-up leaves as sponges.
    c. using stones to crack open nuts.
    *d. All of the above.

22. Jane Goodall's studies of chimpanzees showed that they would often strip leaves off of a branch in order to use it for
    *a. termite "fishing."
    b. hitting one another over the head.
    c. a spear for hunting small monkeys.
    d. building a simple hut.

23. Studies of tool use among chimpanzees shows that these behaviors
    a. are instinctual—all chimp groups practice them.
    b. all resulted from imitating humans.
    *c. vary from group to group.
    d. are *not* passed on through learning.

24. What can be said after comparing chimpanzee and bonobo tool use?
    a. Both chimpanzees and bonobos use tools.
    b. Bonobos use tools, but chimpanzees don't.
    *c. Chimpanzees use tools, but bonobos don't.
    d. Neither chimpanzees nor bonobos use tools.

25. What is the difference between human and chimpanzee tool use?
    a. Humans rely on tools for survival.
    b. Humans save their tools for later use.
    c. Humans use tools to make other tools.
    *d. All of the above.

26. Early attempts to teach apes spoken English failed because the apes
    *a. could not make the same sounds as humans.
    b. lacked sufficient intelligence.
    c. were too young.
    d. killed the scientists.

27. Attempts to teach sign language to apes have demonstrated that
    a. apes are incapable of learning a symbolic language.
    b. apes use sign language only in their native habitat.
    *c. apes can generalize the meaning of signs.
    d. apes prefer to communicate with each other using sign language.

28. As concerns language, the term "displacement" refers to
    a. changes in the vocal anatomy of humans during the growth process.
    b. vocalizations used in dominance disputes.
    *c. discussing events distant in time and/or space.
    d. nouns and verbs relating to human aggression.

29. Human languages are characterized by
    a. being open systems.
    b. having displacement.
    c. being arbitrary.
    *d. All of the above.

30. Washoe was the first chimpanzee to be taught
    *a. American Sign Language.
    b. spoken English.
    c. language using a computer keyboard.
    d. language using plastic symbol tiles.

31. The language acquisition abilities of the bonobo chimpanzee Kanzi are particularly remarkable because
    a. he was very old when the study began.
    b. he hated human beings.
    *c. he learned by observation and not direct teaching.
    d. his mother taught him.

32. Several scientists have attempted to teach Kanzi, a bonobo, how to make stone tools. What happened?
    a. He could make them, and they were better than those made by early humans.
    *b. He could make them, but not as well as early humans.
    c. He could make them, and they were equal in quality to those made by early humans.
    d. He could not make them.

Essay Questions

33. Is the difference between ape and human toolmaking a difference in "degree" or "kind"? Defend your answer.

34. Is the difference between ape and human language acquisition a difference in "degree" or "kind"? Defend your answer.

35. What are the unique features of human growth? How do they differ from other mammals, and why?

CHAPTER 6

PRIMATE ORIGINS AND EVOLUTION

Overview

This chapter focuses on primate origins and evolution. The first part of the chapter provides some needed background before dealing with primate origins—a brief discussion of methods of fossil analysis and a brief review of evolutionary events preceding the first primates. The chapter then reviews primate evolution from the time of primate origins through the end of the Miocene epoch and the ape-human split. The emphasis here is on viewing primate evolution as a series of adaptive radiations. The major events discussed are primate origins, anthropoid origins, and Miocene hominoid diversity. The evolutionary relationships between humans and apes are discussed using fossil and molecular dating evidence.

Outline

I. The Fossil Record
    A. Dating Methods
        1. Relative dating methods
        2. Chronometric dating methods
    B. Reconstructing the Past
        1. Taphonomy
        2. Paleoecology

II. Evolution Before the Primates
    A. The Origin of Life
    B. The Paleozoic Era
    C. The Mesozoic Era

III. Early Primate Evolution
    A. Overview of Early Primate Evolution
    B. Primate Origins
        1. Continental drift and primate evolution
        2. The primatelike mammals
        3. Models of primate origins
        4. The first primates
    C. Anthropoid Origins
        1. Old World anthropoids
        2. Evolution of the New World monkeys

IV. Evolution of the Miocene Apes
  A. The Diversity of Miocene Apes
  B. The Fossil Evidence
    1. *Proconsul*
    2. *Sivapithecus*
  C. Genetic Evidence
  D. Conclusions

V. Summary

VI. Supplemental Readings

  Special Topic: Killer from the Sky?
  Special Topic: The Giant Ape

Topics for Discussion

1. Discuss the vastness of geologic time using Sagan's "Cosmic Calendar" or a similar analogy. One idea is to compress the earth's history relative to a 20-year-old student's life.

2. Discuss the historical controversy over Miocene apes (*Ramapithecus*) being hominids, including the reevaluation of the fossil evidence and the interpretations based on molecular dating.

3. Prior to lecturing on *Sivapithecus*, show students casts or pictures of the Pakistani specimen along with cranial and dental remains of modern chimpanzees and orangutans. Have them draw their own conclusions regarding similarities.

4. Discuss problems of parallelism that arise when considering the evolutionary relationships between chimpanzees, gorillas, and humans.

Multiple-Choice Questions

Correct answers are marked with an asterisk (*). There are multiple questions for certain topics.

1. Primate evolution took place during the
  a. Precambrian eon.
  b. Paleozoic era.
  c. Mesozoic era.
  *d. Cenozoic era.

2. The first primates evolved from primitive
   *a. insectivores.
   b. herbivores.
   c. rodents.
   d. bovines.

3. Continental drift
   a. is genetic drift over large continental regions.
   *b. refers to the process by which the continents move.
   c. is the process by which animal populations drift apart as part of an adaptive radiation.
   d. is a dance step popularized by the Drifters.

4. The primatelike mammals have been found in
   a. Asia and Africa.
   b. Europe and Africa.
   *c. Europe and North America.
   d. Europe and Asia.

5. _____ is a relative dating method.
   a. Carbon-14
   *b. Stratigraphy
   c. Potassium-argon
   d. Argon-argon

6. The principle of stratigraphy shows
   a. which fossil is found at a deeper level—that one is younger.
   *b. which fossil is found at a deeper level—that one is older.
   c. the difference in concentration of fluorine.
   d. similarities in faunal distribution with sites of known age.

7. Faunal correlation is used to date sites by
   a. determining the relative amount of fluorine in the bones.
   b. comparing carbon-14 dates from different animal bones.
   *c. comparing the distribution of animal remains to those from sites of known age.
   d. determining which bones are found at deeper levels.

8. Carbon-14 dating makes use of the rate of decay from
   a. carbon-14 to carbon-12.
   *b. carbon-14 to nitrogen-14.
   c. carbon-12 to carbon-14.
   d. nitrogen-14 to carbon-14.

9. "Half life" refers to
   *a. the time it takes for half of the radioactive isotope in an object to decay into another form.
   b. middle age.
   c. 2.3 billion years.
   d. the time it takes for half of a species to reproduce.

10. _____ dating is useful for dating sites that are millions of years old.
    a. Fluorine
    b. Carbon-14
    *c. Potassium-argon
    d. Dendrochronology

11. Volcanic rock can be dated using _____ dating.
    a. fluorine
    *b. potassium-argon
    c. carbon-14
    d. paleomagnetic reversal

12. Paleomagnetic reversal allows dating by making use of the fact that
    a. intense heat changes a rock's degree of magnetism.
    b. many organisms are drawn to regions of intense magnetism.
    c. the magnetic strength of the magnetic North Pole was greater in the past.
    *d. the earth's magnetic poles have switched at various times in the past.

13. _____ is the study of what happens to plants and animals after they die.
    a. Paleoecology
    *b. Taphonomy
    c. Faunal correlation
    d. Taxonomy

14. Palynology allows reconstruction of ancient environments through the analysis of fossil
    a. bones.
    b. trees.
    c. feces.
    *d. pollen.

15. The earth is _____ years old.
    a. 65 million
    b. 545 million
    c. 3.5 billion
    *d. 4.6 billion

16. The origin of life took place during the
    *a. Precambrian eon.
    b. Phanerozoic eon.
    c. Paleozoic era.
    d. Mesozoic era.

17. The oldest fossils (single-celled organisms) date to _____ years.
    a. 65 million
    b. 545 million
    *c. 3.5 billion
    d. 4.6 billion

18. The vertebrates first appear during the
    a. Precambrian eon.
    *b. Paleozoic era.
    c. Mesozoic era.
    d. Cenozoic era.

19. The earliest vertebrates were the
    a. birdlike reptiles.
    b. mammallike reptiles.
    *c. jawless fish.
    d. dinosaurs.

20. Recent evidence suggests that some early fish (the genus *Acanthostega*) had
    a. an expanded brain.
    *b. legs.
    c. mammalian teeth.
    d. an extra set of fins.

21. Early reptiles first appear during the
    a. Precambrian eon.
    *b. Paleozoic era.
    c. Mesozoic era.
    d. Cenozoic era.

22. What mammal characteristic is seen in the mammallike reptiles?
    a. able to maintain a constant body temperature
    b. fur or hair
    *c. different types of teeth
    d. development of a placenta

23. The _____ is also known as the "Age of Reptiles."
    a. Precambrian eon
    b. Paleozoic era
    *c. Mesozoic era
    d. Cenozoic era

24. The _____ were the dominant life form on land during the Mesozoic era.
    *a. dinosaurs
    b. mammallike reptiles
    c. birdlike reptiles
    d. jawless fish

25. What impact did the extinction of the dinosaurs (65 million years ago) have on the evolution of the mammals?
    a. The mammals became extinct.
    b. The mammals caused the extinction of the dinosaurs.
    c. The remaining dinosaur species interbred with the mammals.
    *d. Many environments, formerly occupied by the dinosaurs, were now available for the mammals.

26. The primatelike mammals lived during the _____ epoch.
    *a. Paleocene
    b. Eocene
    c. Oligocene
    d. Miocene

27. Which of the following primate characteristics is found in the primatelike mammals?
    a. reduction in size of the snout
    b. diurnal adaptation
    c. a postorbital bar
    *d. some grasping ability

28. According to the visual predation model, _____ evolved for hunting _____.
    *a. depth perception / hunting insects
    b. grasping hands / other primates
    c. depth perception / birds
    d. grasping hands / other primates

29. In addition to primates, stereoscopic vision is also found in
    a. whales.
    b. rodents.
    c. cats and dogs.
    *d. cats and some birds.

30. Several models have been proposed to explain the origin of primate characteristics, including
    a. adaptation to an arboreal environment.
    b. hunting insects.
    c. more efficient gathering of fruit.
    *d. All of the above.

31. The first "true primates" appeared during the _____ epoch.
    a. Paleocene
    *b. Eocene
    c. Oligocene
    d. Miocene

32. Eocene primates have been found in
    a. Asia and Africa.
    b. Europe and Africa.
    *c. Europe and North America.
    d. Europe and Asia.

33. Compared to the primatelike mammals, the Eocene primates
    *a. had smaller snouts.
    b. did not have a postorbital bar.
    c. were bipedal.
    d. did not have tails.

34. An adaptive radiation of early anthropoids occurred during the _____ epoch.
    a. Paleocene
    b. Eocene
    *c. Oligocene
    d. Miocene

35. Oligocene anthropoids are found
    *a. in both the Old World and the New World.
    b. only in the Old World.
    c. only in the New World.
    d. in Antarctica.

36. The oldest evidence of New World monkeys is roughly _____ million years ago.
    a. 50
    *b. 30
    c. 15
    d. 5

37. Current evidence suggests that the New World monkeys
    a. did not initially have tails.
    *b. "rafted" from Africa to South America.
    c. evolved independently from New World prosimians.
    d. came to the New World aboard Columbus' ships.

38. The first fossil apes are found during the _____ epoch.
    a. Paleocene
    b. Eocene
    c. Oligocene
    *d. Miocene

39. The climate became _____ during the Miocene epoch.
    a. cooler and wetter
    *b. cooler and drier
    c. hotter and wetter
    d. hotter and drier

40. _____ apes live today than lived between 10 and 20
    million years ago.
    *a. Fewer
    b. More
    c. Just as many
    d. None of the above.

41. _____ is an example of the earliest fossil ape.
    a. *Sivapithecus*
    b. *Aegyptopithecus*
    *c. *Proconsul*
    d. *Gigantopithecus*

42. *Proconsul* lived in
    a. Asia roughly 20 million years ago.
    b. Africa roughly 50 million years ago.
    *c. Africa roughly 20 million years ago.
    d. Africa roughly 50 million years ago.

43. *Proconsul* had _____, which is a characteristic of modern
    apes, and _____, which is a characteristic of modern
    monkeys.
    *a. no tail / front and rear limbs of equal length
    b. front limbs longer than rear limbs / a tail
    c. no tail / front limbs longer than rear limbs
    d. front and rear limbs of equal length / a tail

44. How is *Proconsul* similar to living apes?
    a. It had very small canines (human size).
    b. It was a knuckle walker.
    c. The arms were longer than the legs.
    *d. It did not have a tail.

45. How is *Proconsul* similar to living monkeys?
    *a. Its arms were roughly the same length as its legs.
    b. It had a tail.
    c. A and B.
    d. None of the above.

46. *Sivapithecus* lived in _____ between 14 and 7 million years ago.
    a. Africa and Asia
    *b. Asia and Europe
    c. Europe and Africa
    d. Africa, Asia, and Europe

47. The teeth of *Sivapithecus* are different from those of *Proconsul* and other early apes. *Sivapithecus* has
    a. relatively large molars.
    b. jaws that do not protrude as much as in other apes.
    c. thick molar enamel.
    *d. All of the above.

48. If you do a lot of chewing of tough material, you are better off if
    a. your canines are larger.
    *b. your canines are smaller.
    c. you have extra canines.
    d. someone else chews your food for you.

49. The facial structure of some species of *Sivapithecus* suggests that they might be the ancestor of the modern
    a. baboon.
    b. gibbon.
    *c. orangutan.
    d. African apes.

50. Oval-shaped eye orbits are a feature found in modern _____ as well as certain species of *Sivapithecus*.
    a. chimpanzees
    b. gorillas
    *c. orangutans
    d. gibbons

51. Molecular dating suggests that humans and apes diverged from a common ancestor roughly _____ million years ago.
    a. 2 to 3
    *b. 5 to 7
    c. 10 to 15
    d. 15 to 20

52. Imagine that you are studying three living species (A, B, and C). Suppose species C is known to have split from the common ancestor of A and B 60 million years ago. Also suppose that we know the genetic distance between species A and B is one-tenth that of the genetic distance between species A and C (or B and C). According to the method of molecular dating, we can estimate that species A and B split from a common ancestor _____ million years ago.
    *a. 6
    b. 10
    c. 20
    d. 30

53. What can we say about the common ancestor of the human and African ape lines?
    *a. We have several good candidates, but we can't pick the best one at present.
    b. There is absolutely no fossil evidence for such a split.
    c. The common ancestor was definitely *Kenyapithecus*.
    d. The common ancestor was definitely *Proconsul*.

54. *Gigantopithecus*
    a. was a large Miocene ape that walked upright.
    b. was at least 20 feet tall.
    *c. had exceptionally large molar teeth.
    d. was a giant ape that died fighting the dinosaurs.

Essay Questions

55. Discuss the arboreal and visual predation hypotheses of primate origins. How could fossil data be used to test these hypotheses?

56. What was *Proconsul*? Describe its anatomy and evolutionary relationships to later hominoids.

57. What was *Sivapithecus*? Describe its anatomy and evolutionary relationships to later hominoids.

58. What is molecular dating? How has it been used to address issues of human origins?

CHAPTER 7

HUMAN ORIGINS

Overview

This chapter, the first of three (7–9) focusing on human evolution, covers the fossil evidence and models of evolution relating to Plio-Pleistocene hominid evolution. The chapter begins with a brief summary of human evolution. The general characteristics of the australopithecines (and *Ardipithecus*) are covered, followed by an examination of the biology and behavior of *Homo habilis*. The remainder of the chapter deals with models of early hominid evolution, including consideration of possible evolutionary relationships, the origin of bipedalism, and the origin of brain expansion and stone tool technology.

Outline

I.   Overview of Human Evolution

II. The First Hominids
    A. Early Species
        1. *Ardipithecus ramidus*
        2. The genus *Australopithecus*
        3. *Australopithecus anamensis*
        4. *Australopithecus afarensis*
    B. Later Australopithecines
        1. Robust australopithecines
        2. *Australopithecus africanus*

III. *Homo habilis*
    A. General Physical Characteristics
        1. Brain size
        2. Teeth
        3. The skeleton
    B. Behavior
        1. Stone tool technology
        2. Hunting or scavenging?
        3. Home bases?

IV. Evolutionary Trends
   A. Evolutionary Relationships
   B. The Origin of Bipedalism
       1. The tool use model
       2. Predator avoidance
       3. Reproductive success
       4. Food acquisition
       5. Temperature regulation
   C. The Increase in Brain Size
       1. Neoteny
       2. Advantages of larger brains
       3. The radiator theory

V. Summary

VI. Supplemental Readings

   Special Topic: The Piltdown Hoax

Topics for Discussion

1. As an example of the problems faced with identification of fossil species, mix up a number of Plio-Pleistocene hominid casts (or pictures) with several other forms (e.g., modern apes and humans). Have students decide how many species they see.

2. Discuss both the advantages and disadvantages of large brains. Relate this to a general discussion of relative costs and benefits (i.e., is there such a thing as a "free lunch"?).

3. What can we actually say about the behavior of *Homo habilis*? What else can we infer? Can various ideas be tested? How?

4. Discuss how a single specimen (e.g., ER 1470 or WT 17000) can lead to new interpretations while not actually changing our general picture of human evolution.

Multiple-Choice Questions

Correct answers are marked with an asterisk (*). There are multiple questions for certain topics.

1. Hominids include species in the genera
   *a. *Ardipithecus, Australopithecus,* and *Homo.*
   b. *Australopithecus* and *Homo* (not *Ardipithecus*).
   c. *Ardipthecus* and *Australopithecus* (not *Homo*).
   d. *Ardipithecus* and *Homo* (not *Australopithecus*).

2. The oldest known hominid species, dating to 4.4 million years B.P., is
   a. *Australopithecus afarensis.*
   *b. *Ardipithecus ramidus.*
   c. *Australopithecus anamensis.*
   d. *Australopithecus africanus.*

3. Fossil hominids are found during the
   a. Pliocene epoch.
   *b. Pliocene and Pleistocene epochs.
   c. Pleistocene epoch.
   d. Miocene, Pliocene, and Pleistocene epochs.

4. The first hominids are found in
   a. Asia.
   b. Europe.
   c. the New World.
   *d. Africa.

5. The most primitive hominids are
   *a. *Ardipithecus ramidus, Australopithecus anamensis,* and *Australopithecus afarensis.*
   b. *Ardipithecus ramidus, Australopithecus anamensis,* and *Homo habilis.*
   c. *Australopithecus anamensis, Homo habilis,* and the robust australopithecines.
   d. *Homo habilis* and *Homo sapiens.*

6. The newly discovered fossil *Ardipithecus* appears to be
   a. an extinct species of chimpanzee.
   b. the oldest known direct ancestor of modern humans (following the split of ape and hominid lines).
   *c. an early hominid, but not a direct ancestor of later hominids.
   d. an extinct species of monkey.

7. The genus name *Australopithecus* translates as
    a. "Australian ape."
    *b. "southern ape."
    c. "Australian monkey."
    d. "southern monkey."

8. _____ lived 4.2 to 3.9 million years ago, and is the oldest known hominid species that is directly ancestral to modern humans.
    a. *Ardipithecus ramidus*
    *b. *Australopithecus anamensis*
    c. *Australopithecus afarensis*
    d. *Homo habilis*

9. *Australopithecus afarensis* lived roughly _____ million years ago.
    a. 2.5 to 1
    b. 3 to 2
    c. 2.5 to 1.5
    *d. 4 to 3

10. The fossil known as "Lucy" belongs to the species
    a. *Australopithecus anamensis.*
    *b. *Australopithecus afarensis.*
    c. *Australopithecus africanus.*
    d. *Homo habilis.*

11. *Australopithecus afarensis*
    a. was completely identical to modern humans in terms of bipedal anatomy.
    *b. was a biped, but retained considerable climbing ability.
    c. was a quadruped that occasionally walked upright.
    d. was most likely an occasional knuckle walker.

12. The canine teeth of *Australopithecus afarensis* are
    a. larger than modern apes.
    b. smaller than modern humans.
    *c. smaller than modern apes, but larger than modern humans.
    d. the same size as modern humans.

13. The premolars of *Australopithecus afarensis* are
    a. identical to modern monkeys.
    b. identical to modern apes.
    c. identical to modern humans.
    *d. intermediate in structure between modern apes and modern humans.

14. Imagine you have found a skull with an ape-size brain, very large back teeth, and large cheekbones. Based on this information, this is most likely a specimen of
    a. *Australopithecus afarensis.*
    *b. robust australopithecine.
    c. *Homo habilis.*
    d. modern human.

15. The three species of robust australopithecine are
    a. *Australopithecus afarensis, Australopithecus africanus,* and *Australopithecus robustus.*
    b. *Australopithecus africanus, Australopithecus robustus,* and *Australopithecus boisei.*
    c. *Australopithecus afarensis, Australopithecus robustus,* and *Australopithecus boisei.*
    *d. *Australopithecus robustus, Australopithecus boisei,* and *Australopithecus aethiopicus.*

16. The robust australopithecines lived roughly _____ million years ago.
    *a. 2.5 to 1
    b. 3 to 2
    c. 2.5 to 1.5
    d. 4 to 3

17. Compared to other hominid species, the robust australopithecines have relatively
    a. smaller front teeth and smaller back teeth.
    b. larger front teeth and larger back teeth.
    c. larger front teeth and smaller back teeth.
    *d. smaller front teeth and larger back teeth.

18. The large teeth, jaws, and chewing muscles of the robust australopithecines reflects adaptation to
    *a. a hard diet.
    b. a high altitude environment.
    c. meat eating.
    d. defense against carnivores.

19. A sagittal crest is frequently found in
    a. *Australopithecus afarensis.*
    *b. the robust australopithecines.
    c. *Australopithecus africanus.*
    d. *Homo habilis.*

20. The sagittal crest functions to
    a. anchor neck muscles.
    *b. anchor chewing muscles.
    c. anchor leg muscles.
    d. increase the attractiveness of male hominids.

21. _____ shows a number of traits that link it to
    Australopithecus afarensis and to later robust australopithecines.
    a. *Australopithecus africanus*
    b. *Australopithecus robustus*
    *c. *Australopithecus aethiopicus*
    d. *Australopithecus anamensis*

22. The robust australopithecines
    *a. became extinct roughly one million years ago.
    b. evolved into *Homo habilis*.
    c. evolved into *Homo erectus*.
    d. left Africa roughly one million years ago.

23. *Australopithecus africanus* lived roughly _____ million years ago.
    a. 2.5 to 1
    *b. 3 to 2
    c. 2.5 to 1.5
    d. 4 to 3

24. *Australopithecus africanus* is possibly an ancestor of
    a. *Homo habilis*.
    b. *Australopithecus robustus*.
    c. *Australopithecus afarensis*.
    *d. A and B.

25. *Homo habilis* lived roughly _____ million years ago.
    a. 2.5 to 1
    b. 3 to 2
    *c. 2.5 to 1.5
    d. 4 to 3

26. The brain size of *Homo habilis* is
    a. equal to modern apes.
    b. equal to modern humans.
    *c. roughly one-half the size of modern humans.
    d. roughly 3/4 the size of modern humans.

27. Imagine you found a skull in Africa, with a brain roughly half the size of an average modern human, and dating to 2 million years B.P. Based on this information, this is most likely a specimen of
   a. *Australopithecus afarensis.*
   b. *Australopithecus africanus.*
   *c. *Homo habilis.*
   d. *Homo erectus.*

28. The wide range in anatomical variation seen in *Homo habilis* has been interpreted as
   a. sex differences in size.
   b. indicating more than one species.
   *c. A and B.
   d. None of the above.

29. Analysis of *Homo habilis* endocasts suggests that
   *a. their brain structure was more similar to modern humans than to modern apes.
   b. they frequently climbed trees.
   c. they were meat eaters.
   d. some left Africa by two million years ago.

30. Compared to earlier hominids, the teeth of *Homo habilis* are
   a. larger.
   *b. smaller.
   c. fewer in number.
   d. greater in number.

31. The Oldowan culture is associated with
   *a. *Homo habilis.*
   b. *Homo erectus.*
   c. *Homo sapiens.*
   d. *Australopithecus africanus.*

32. Archaeological evidence suggests that *Homo habilis* made use of _____ as a food source.
   a. hunting and gathering.
   *b. scavenging of dead animals.
   c. other hominids.
   d. only plant and vegetable matter.

33. Which of the following *definitely* made stone tools?
   a. *Australopithecus afarensis*
   b. *Australopithecus africanus*
   c. the robust australopithecines
   *d. *Homo habilis*

34. What did *Homo habilis* use animal bones for?
   *a. They cracked them open and ate the marrow.
   b. digging implements
   c. Large bones were used as support for crude shelters.
   d. weapons

35. Recent investigations of early stone tools suggest that the small flakes produced by chipping
   a. are garbage left over from shaping the stone core.
   *b. were used for a variety of cutting tasks.
   c. were often picked up by chimpanzees later on to use for cutting branches for termite fishing.
   d. were used to kill one another (slitting of throats while they were asleep).

36. Bipedalism first evolved in
   *a. Africa.
   b. Europe.
   c. Asia.
   d. Australasia.

37. The tool-use model of hominid origins has been rejected because
   a. of the Black Skull specimen.
   *b. bipedalism existed long before stone tools were used.
   c. an increase in brain size began at roughly the same time as the origin of stone tools.
   d. some australopithecines had longer canines.

38. Bipedalism appears to have been originally selected for, in part, because
   a. the earliest hominids needed to carry stone tools.
   b. it provided the greatest running speed.
   c. the arms were free for climbing trees.
   *d. it provided greater energy efficiency for long distance movement.

39. Lovejoy's model, which focuses on reproductive advantage, suggests that bipedalism evolved
   a. to carry weapons and tools.
   b. to run away from predators, such as jungle cats.
   *c. to facilitate transport of food back to females and infants.
   d. to avoid heat stress.

40. According to Wheeler, who looked at the relationship of posture and temperature regulation,
    a. there is less cold stress when an organism is bipedal.
    b. there is less cold stress when an organism is on all fours.
    *c. there is less heat stress when an organism is bipedal.
    d. there is less heat stress when an organism is on all fours.

41. Neoteny is
    a. the origin of new evolutionary adaptations.
    *b. the retention of juvenile characteristics into adulthood.
    c. the evolution of ten digits on hands (and feet).
    d. None of the above.

42. The skull shape of modern chimpanzees and humans
    *a. looks more similar in infants than in adults.
    b. looks more similar in adults than in infants.
    c. looks more similar in adolescence than in infancy or adulthood.
    d. looks totally different throughout their lives.

43. Falk's radiator theory is based in part on the observation that two forms of _____ have been discovered among early hominids.
    *a. cranial blood drainage systems
    b. bipedalism
    c. sagittal crests
    d. language areas in the brain

44. According to Falk's radiator theory, a major disadvantage of larger brains is
    *a. overheating.
    b. the need for greater energy (food).
    c. difficult childbirth.
    d. the development of language.

45. Early models of hominid origins focused on the idea that large brains came first. This idea was supported by a find known as _____, that was later shown to be a hoax.
    a. Lucy
    b. the Black Skull
    *c. Piltdown
    d. ER-1470

Essay Questions

46. Describe the tool use model of the origin of bipedalism and explain what fossil evidence led to its rejection.

47. What is neoteny, and how does it relate to human evolution?

48. What does the anatomy of the first primitive hominids tell us about the nature of evolutionary transitions?

49. In terms of behavior, how is *Homo habilis* similar to us? How is it different? What does this tell you about the difference between "hominid," "human," and "modern human"?

CHAPTER 8

THE EVOLUTION OF THE GENUS *HOMO*

Overview

This chapter covers the fossil and archaeological evidence for the evolution of *Homo erectus* and "archaic" *Homo sapiens* (which includes the Neandertals). Both are discussed in terms of geographic and temporal distribution, basic physical characteristics, and cultural behaviors. The transition to modern *Homo sapiens* is covered in the next chapter.

Outline

I. *Homo erectus*
   A. Distribution in Time and Space
   B. General Physical Characteristics
     1. Brain size
     2. Cranial and dental characteristics
     3. The postcranial skeleton
   C. Cultural Behavior
     1. Stone tool technology
     2. Hunting and gathering
     3. Fire

II. Archaic *Homo sapiens*
   A. Distribution in Time and Space
   B. Physical Characteristics
     1. Regional variation
     2. The Neandertals
   C. Cultural Behavior
     1. Stone tool technology
     2. Symbolic behavior

III. Summary

IV. Supplemental Readings

   Special Topic: Neandertals: Names and Images

Topics for Discussion

1. Discuss gradualism and punctuated equilibrium with respect to the evolution of brain size in *Homo erectus*. How conclusive are the data?

2. Show a film on hunters and gatherers (e.g., *The Hunters*). Discuss problems in extrapolating the behavior of modern hunters and gatherers to early hominids.

3. Discuss changing interpretations of "man the hunter," "woman the gatherer," and "humans the food sharers" and how they are affected by current cultural context.

4. Show parts of a film dealing with Neandertals (e.g., *Clan of the Cave Bear, Quest for Fire*). Have the students identify errors.

Multiple-Choice Questions

Correct answers are marked with an asterisk (*). There are multiple questions for certain topics.

1. *Homo erectus* has been found
   a. only in Africa.
   b. in Africa and Europe.
   c. in Europe and Asia.
   *d. in Africa and Asia (and possibly Europe).

2. The earliest known specimens of *Homo erectus* are dated to _____ million years B.P.
   a. 1.2
   *b. 1.8
   c. 2.5
   d. 3.0

3. The first hominid to leave Africa was
   a. *Homo habilis.*
   *b. *Homo erectus.*
   c. archaic *Homo sapiens.*
   d. anatomically modern *Homo sapiens.*

4. New evidence suggests that *Homo erectus* may have reached Indonesia by _____ million years B.P.
   a. 0.2
   b. 0.5
   c. 1.0
   *d. 1.7

5. New dating of *Homo erectus* sites in Indonesia suggests that *Homo erectus*
   *a. left Africa shortly after its initial origin.
   b. did not leave Africa until roughly one million years ago.
   c. evolved first in Asia, and then later spread into Africa.
   d. never left Africa.

6. Definite evidence for *Homo erectus* in Europe is complicated by the fact that
   a. the Neandertals may have ground up *Homo erectus* bones in their rituals, leaving little for us to discover.
   b. Europe was separate from Asia during this time (because of continental drift).
   *c. most of the evidence consists of stone tools that were also made by early *Homo sapiens*.
   d. new dates from Indonesia are much earlier than once suspected.

7. The large brow ridges seen in *Homo erectus* and archaic *Homo sapiens* are due to
   a. a birth defect that spread throughout these species because of genetic drift.
   *b. stresses imposed by chewing muscles and neck muscles.
   c. an adaptation arising to protect the eyes from rain.
   d. sexual selection; that is, those individuals with larger brow ridges were considered more attractive, and hence reproduced more often than those with small brow ridges.

8. The brain size of *Homo erectus* is
   a. equal to modern apes.
   b. equal to modern humans.
   c. roughly one-half the size of modern humans.
   *d. roughly 3/4 the size of modern humans.

9. The *Homo erectus* skeleton of a 12-year old boy shows that *Homo erectus*
   a. had smaller pelvic dimensions than modern humans.
   b. had body proportions similar to modern humans.
   c. was rather tall.
   *d. All of the above.

10. Compared with modern humans, the skull of *Homo erectus* is characterized by
   a. smaller brain size.
   b. a protruding face.
   c. post-orbital constriction.
   *d. All of the above.

11. The tools known as hand axes are associated with
    a. *Homo habilis.*
    *b. *Homo erectus.*
    c. archaic *Homo sapiens.*
    d. anatomically modern *Homo sapiens.*

12. The Acheulian tradition is associated with
    a. *Homo habilis.*
    *b. *Homo erectus.*
    c. archaic *Homo sapiens.*
    d. anatomically modern *Homo sapiens.*

13. Chopping tools are found with *Homo erectus* populations in
    a. Africa.
    b. Europe.
    *c. Asia.
    d. All of the above.

14. Geographic analysis suggests that *Homo erectus* in Asia often relied on _____ for tools.
    a. animal bones
    b. sea shells
    *c. bamboo
    d. plastic

15. *Homo erectus* was the first hominid species to
    *a. hunt.
    b. scavenge dead animals.
    c. farm.
    d. worship cave bears.

16. The oldest known use of fire is associated with
    a. *Homo habilis.*
    *b. *Homo erectus.*
    c. archaic *Homo sapiens.*
    d. anatomically modern *Homo sapiens.*

17. The greatest proportion of calories in a hunting and gathering society comes from
    a. hunting (small game).
    b. hunting (large game).
    c. hunting (any size game).
    *d. gathering.

18. The earliest known use of fire dates to roughly _____ years ago.
    a. 50,000
    b. 300,000
    *c. one million
    d. two million

19. The *Homo erectus* site at Zhoukoudian, China contains evidence of
    a. use of fire.
    b. hunting.
    c. use of caves for shelter.
    *d. All of the above.

20. Archaic *Homo sapiens* has been found in
    a. Africa.
    b. Asia.
    c. Europe.
    *d. All of the above.

21. Who had the biggest brain?
    a. the robust australopithecines
    b. *Homo habilis*
    c. *Homo erectus*
    *d. archaic *Homo sapiens*

22. Neandertals are _____ *Homo sapiens* that lived in _____.
    a. archaic / Africa
    *b. archaic / Europe and the Middle East
    c. modern / Africa
    d. modern / Europe and the Middle East

23. The cranial capacity of _____ and _____ is *roughly* the same.
    a. *Homo habilis* / *Homo erectus*
    b. *Homo erectus* / archaic *Homo sapiens*
    *c. archaic *Homo sapiens* / modern *Homo sapiens*
    d. *Australopithecus* / *Homo sapiens*

24. Compared with modern *Homo sapiens*, archaic *Homo sapiens* had
    a. smaller front teeth.
    b. a more well-rounded skull.
    *c. a sloping forehead.
    d. thinner bones.

25. Compared to ourselves, Neandertals
    *a. did not have a chin.
    b. had smaller brains.
    c. did not walk fully upright.
    d. were much taller.

26. Compared to Neandertals, modern humans
    *a. have a higher skull with a more vertical forehead.
    b. have much larger brains.
    c. are more muscular.
    d. have more teeth.

27. Compared to ourselves, archaic *Homo sapiens*
    a. had smaller brains and similar shaped skulls.
    b. had larger brains and similar shaped skulls.
    c. had the same brain size and the same shape of the skull.
    *d. had the same brain size and a differently shaped skull.

28. A distinctive feature of _____ is that they had big noses.
    a. *Homo habilis*
    b. *Homo erectus*
    c. *Australopithecus africanus*
    *d. Neandertals

29. Compared to ourselves, Neandertals had _____ front teeth.
    *a. larger
    b. smaller
    c. more
    d. fewer

30. Many Neandertals possessed a _____, where the back of the skull is puffed out.
    a. sagittal crest
    b. nuchal crest
    *c. occipital bun
    d. foramen magnum

31. The larger _____ of Neandertals may reflect their use as tools.
    a. thumbs
    b. brains
    c. noses
    *d. front teeth

77

32. Compared to modern Europeans, Neandertals were
    a. tall and slender.
    b. taller and more muscular.
    *c. shorter and stockier.
    d. shorter and less muscular.

33. A prepared core technique is first seen in the stone tool tradition of
    a. anatomically modern *Homo sapiens.*
    b. *Homo erectus.*
    *c. archaic *Homo sapiens.*
    d. *Homo habilis.*

34. The "prepared core" method of tool making
    a. is very *inefficient*—it requires more raw material.
    *b. is very *efficient*—it allows more tools to be made from a given amount of raw material.
    c. is useful only for making handaxes.
    d. is used for shaping bamboo knives.

35. The _____ tradition is associated with archaic *Homo sapiens.*
    *a. Mousterian
    b. Acheulian
    c. Oldowan
    d. Solutrean

36. Burial of the dead was first practiced by
    a. *Homo habilis.*
    b. *Homo erectus.*
    *c. archaic *Homo sapiens.*
    d. modern *Homo sapiens.*

37. Fossil pollen found in the graves of Neandertals at the site of Shanidar have been interpreted as suggesting someone put flowers in the grave. Another interpretation is that the pollen was
    a. never there—the whole thing is a fake.
    *b. brought in by burrowing rodents.
    c. rubbed on the bones as part of a ritual.
    d. the result of wrapping the body in giant lettuce leaves.

Essay Questions

38. What are the advantages and disadvantages of using terms such as "archaic" and "modern" *Homo sapiens*?

39. Discuss alternative hypotheses to explain the differences in stone tool technology of African and Asian *Homo erectus*.

40. Who were the Neandertals? Where and when did they live, what did they look like, and how did they live?

CHAPTER 9

THE ORIGIN OF MODERN HUMANS

Overview

This chapter examines the fossil and archaeological evidence for anatomically modern *Homo sapiens*. The first part of the chapter examines geographic and temporal distribution, physical characteristics, and cultural behavior (including Upper Paleolithic tools, the first evidence of art, and geographic expansion). The second part of the chapter deals with the current controversy regarding the origin of modern humans (multiregional versus recent African origin/replacement), and examines both fossil and genetic evidence (including some rather new interpretations of the latter). This section also examines different hypotheses regarding *why* modern humans evolved (e.g., loss of robusticity due to replacement by technology, language origins). The chapter concludes with a brief summary of more recent cultural changes (within the last 12,000 years).

Outline

I.   Anatomically Modern *Homo sapiens*
     A. Distribution in Time and Space
     B. Physical Characteristics
     C. Cultural Behavior
        1. Tool technologies
        2. Shelter
        3. Cave art
        4. Other evidence of art
        5. Geographic expansion
        6. Summary of the culture of early modern *Homo sapiens*

II. The Origin of Anatomically Modern *Homo sapiens*
     A. Current Models and Debates
        1. Multiregional model
        2. The recent African origin model
     B. The Fossil Evidence
     C. The Genetic Evidence
        1. Patterns of genetic variation
        2. Population size and modern human origins
        3. A prehistoric population explosion?

Topics for Discussion

1. Discuss problems in interpreting the symbolic meaning of art in ancient populations.

2. Discuss the "lag" between cultural and biological evolution in *Homo sapiens* (i.e., that modern morphology appears at least 50,000 years before most of the cultural changes associated with the "creative explosion").

3. Consider the hypothesis that modern language capabilities first appear in anatomically modern *Homo sapiens*. What type of earlier system of communication might have allowed the development of cultural behaviors among *Homo erectus* and archaic *Homo sapiens*?

4. Discuss the "mitochondrial Eve" debate, focusing on misinterpretations.

Multiple-Choice Questions

Correct answers are marked with an asterisk (*). There are multiple questions for certain topics.

1. Fossil specimens of anatomically modern *Homo sapiens* have been found
   *a. in the Old World and in the New World.
   b. in the Old World only.
   c. in the New World only.
   d. all over the world, excepting Australia.

2. The oldest known specimens of early modern *Homo sapiens* (more than 90,000 years old) have been found in
   a. Europe and Africa.
   b. Europe and Asia.
   *c. Africa and the Middle East.
   d. Australia.

3. Recent fossil evidence suggests that anatomically modern *Homo sapiens* first appeared in _____ perhaps as much as 130,000 years ago.
   *a. Africa
   b. East Asia
   c. Europe
   d. Australia

4. The term "Paleolithic" means
   a. "New Stone Age."
   *b. "Old Stone Age."
   c. "New tools."
   d. "Old tools."

5. Modern *Homo sapiens* are associated with _____ tools.
   *a. Upper Paleolithic
   b. Middle Paleolithic
   c. Lower Paleolithic
   d. None of the above.

6. Blade tools are characterized as
   a. being simple chopping tools.
   *b. being twice as long as wide.
   c. having a serrated edge.
   d. closely resembling Oldowan tools.

7. A burin is a
   a. large prehistoric mammal (similar in size to a mastodon).
   b. small prehistoric rodent.
   *c. stone tool used to etch and engrave bone.
   d. stone tool used to start fires.

8. The use of bone tools was first developed by
   *a. modern *Homo sapiens*.
   b. archaic *Homo sapiens*.
   c. *Homo erectus*.
   d. *Homo habilis*.

9. The oldest known bone tools (found in Africa) date to
   _____ years B.P.
   a. 12,000
   b. 35,000
   *c. 90,000
   d. 200,000

10. The people at Mal'ta used _____ to make shelters.
    a. sticks and leaves
    b. clay
    *c. large animal bones
    d. large stone blocks

11. Cave art first appears with
    *a. modern *Homo sapiens.*
    b. archaic *Homo sapiens.*
    c. *Homo erectus.*
    d. *Homo habilis.*

12. Cave art has been found in
    a. Europe.
    b. Africa.
    c. Australia.
    *d. All of the above.

13. According to the "sympathetic magic" interpretation of cave art,
    the cave pictures represent
    a. the images of gods who have great supernatural powers.
    b. the basic duality of the universe (e.g., male-female, light-
        dark, etc.).
    *c. the desire to capture animals.
    d. the attempt to understand the mind of an animal.

14. The most common themes in prehistoric art are
    a. human disease and fertility.
    b. human disease and dangers of childbirth.
    *c. animals, hunting, and fertility.
    d. exploration of new territories.

15. Venus figures are _____ that are usually interpreted as
    representing _____.
    a. sculptures / successful hunting
    *b. sculptures / fertility
    c. cave paintings / successful hunting
    d. cave paintings / fertility

16. Venus figures are characterized by
    a. extremely detailed faces.
    *b. exaggerated secondary sexual characteristics (e.g., breasts and buttocks).
    c. a lack of arms.
    d. an emphasis on hunting.

17. Recent evidence suggests that modern humans reached Australia via boats roughly _____ years ago.
    a. 10,000
    b. 20,000
    *c. 50,000
    d. over 100,000

18. Although there is some continuing controversy, most archaeologists agree that the earliest known evidence of *Homo sapiens* in the New World dates to roughly _____ years ago.
    a. 5,000–7,000
    *b. 12,000–15,000
    c. 30,000–40,000
    d. over 100,000

19. Humans first reached the Americas by
    *a. crossing the Bering Straits during an ice age.
    b. crossing the North Pole during an ice age.
    c. traveling in boats across the Pacific Ocean.
    d. traveling in boats across the Atlantic Ocean.

20. Genetic, skeletal, and archaeological evidence supports the conclusion that the first Native Americans came from
    *a. Asia.
    b. Europe.
    c. Africa.
    d. Australasia.

21. The multiregional model of modern human origins hypothesizes that modern humans arose
    a. only in Africa.
    b. only in Europe.
    c. only in Asia.
    *d. across the Old World.

22. The recent African origin model suggests that modern humans first evolved in Africa roughly _____ years ago.
    a. 1,000–2,000
    b. 10,000–20,000
    *c. 100,000–200,000
    d. one million to two million

23. The idea that modern *Homo sapiens* appeared first in Africa and then spread out replacing archaic *Homo sapiens* populations throughout the Old World is known as the _____ model.
    a. multiregional
    *b. recent African origin
    c. assimilation
    d. tool-use

24. According to the _____ model, modern Asians should be more similar to archaic Asians than to any other archaic population.
    *a. multiregional
    b. recent African origin
    c. assimilation
    d. tool-use

25. According to the idea of regional continuity, modern Europeans should share certain unique characteristics with archaic
    *a. Europeans.
    b. Africans.
    c. Asians.
    d. Australasians.

26. Anatomically modern *Homo sapiens* appears latest in
    *a. Europe.
    b. Africa.
    c. the Middle East.
    d. Australasia.

27. The strongest evidence for regional continuity occurs in
    a. the New World.
    b. Europe.
    *c. Australasia
    d. the Middle East.

28. The pattern of distribution of Neandertals and modern *Homo sapiens* in the Middle East suggests
    a. a gradual transition from Neandertals to moderns over time.
    b. the invasion and replacement of Neandertals by 100,000 years ago.
    c. no humans ever lived there until the origin of agriculture.
    *d. expansion and contraction of populations as the climate changed.

29. Compared to nuclear DNA, mitochondrial DNA
    a. is inherited from both parents.
    *b. is inherited from the mother.
    c. is inherited from the father.
    d. does not occur in humans.

30. In terms of your mitochondrial DNA, you have _____ ancestors two generations ago.
    *a. 1
    b. 2
    c. 4
    d. 8

31. Among living humans, the greatest genetic diversity is generally found in
    a. Europe.
    *b. Africa.
    c. Asia.
    d. Australasia.

32. Genetic comparisons among living human populations typically show _____ to be the most different.
    a. Europe
    b. Asia
    *c. Africa
    d. Australasia

33. Studies of mitochondrial DNA in living humans generally show a primary division between _____ and _____ populations.
    *a. African and non-African
    b. European and non-European
    c. Asian and non-Asian
    d. None of the above.

34. According to some interpretations of mitochondrial DNA, a common female ancestor of all living humans lived in _____ roughly _____ years ago.
    a. Africa / 1,000,000
    b. Asia / 1,000,000
    *c. Africa / 200,000
    d. Asia / 200,000

35. While the higher genetic diversity in Africa has often been interpreted as support for a recent African origin, another possibility is that
    a. modern humans moved into Africa for the first time roughly 50,000 years ago.
    b. patterns of disease altered the pattern of genetic diversity.
    *c. Africa had a larger population than other regions in the past.
    d. there was a great deal of migration from the New World.

36. Studies of genetic data suggest that the average size of the human species some 100,000 to 200,000 years ago was roughly _____ adults.
    *a. 10,000
    b. 100,000
    c. 1,000,000
    d. 10,000,000

37. Recent analyses of mitochondrial DNA show that our species experienced _____ roughly 40,000 to 60,000 years ago.
    a. evolutionary stasis
    *b. rapid population growth
    c. a series of local extinctions
    d. contact with creatures from other planets

38. Some anthropologists view changes in symbolic behavior as having occurred at the same time as the origin of
    a. modern brain size.
    b. bipedalism.
    c. tool use.
    *d. language.

39. Modern humans
    *a. have their larynx lower in the throat than apes.
    b. have their larynx higher in the throat than apes.
    c. have the same vocal anatomy as apes.
    d. do not have a larynx.

40. Studies by Laitman and colleagues suggest that the vocal anatomy of _____ was different than that of modern humans.
    *a. Neandertals (but not other archaics)
    b. all archaics
    c. all archaics (except Neandertals)
    d. Cro-Magnon

41. The evolution from archaic to modern *Homo sapiens* involved a reduction in skeletal robusticity, suggesting that
    a. there were many neutral mutations that affected growth hormone secretion.
    b. modern forms appeared first in Africa.
    c. there was a significant change in diet.
    *d. the previous advantage of rugged bones and greater musculature was replaced by technology.

42. Agriculture first began roughly _____ years ago.
    a. 2,000
    *b. 12,000
    c. 200,000
    d. 1,500,000

43. Recent evidence on the origin of agriculture suggests that
    a. the first agricultural populations were very large, and then became somewhat smaller.
    b. the transition to agriculture took place within a decade.
    d. it took over 100,000 years for agriculture to spread over the Old World and the New World.
    *d. population pressure led to the full development of agriculture.

44. Agriculture originated
    a. in the Middle East and spread throughout the rest of the world.
    b. in Asia and spread throughout the rest of the world.
    c. in Africa and spread throughout the rest of the world.
    *d. in many places around the world independently.

Essay Questions

45. Describe briefly the multiregional and recent African origin models for the origin of modern humans. How are they similar? How are they different?

46. Describe the alternative hypotheses for the finding that, among living humans, sub-Saharan Africans have the greatest genetic diversity and are also the most genetically divergent.

47. Discuss possible reasons for the observed reduction in the size of the face and teeth in humans over the past 200,000 years.

CHAPTER 10

THE STUDY OF HUMAN VARIATION

Overview

This chapter is the first of three (10–12) that deals with human biological variation. The current chapter provides an introduction to the study of human variation by describing the methods and models for analysis. The chapter begins with a brief survey of the different ways in which human variation can be measured. The chapter then discusses the "race" concept, and how it has been misused and how it is inappropriate for the study of human biological variation. The chapter concludes with a discussion of the evolutionary approach to the study of variation, including some specific methods used for examining biological variation in human populations.

Outline

I. Measuring Human Variation
   A. Biochemical Variation
      1. Blood types
      2. Other genetic traits
   B. Complex Trait Variation
      1. Anthropometrics
      2. Skin color
      3. Other measures

II. The Racial Approach to Variation
   A. The Biological Concept of Race
   B. Problems with the Concept of Race
      1. The number of human races
      2. The nature of continuous variation
      3. Correspondence of different traits
      4. Variation between and within groups
      5. What use is the race concept?

III. The Evolutionary Approach to Variation
   A. The Analysis of Gene Flow and Genetic Drift
      1. Genetic distance analysis
      2. Demographic measures

B. The Analysis of Natural Selection
1. Individual genetic associations
2. Environmental correspondence
3. Demographic measures
4. Problems in analysis

IV. Summary

V. Supplemental Readings

Special Topic: Genetics, Race, and IQ

Topics for Discussion

1. Present slides of people from a number of different regions and cultures and have the students try to assign each a "race." Discuss the problems encountered in their classifications.

2. Show students a set of objects showing a continuous range of variation (different colors of nail polish or lipstick are useful here) and ask them to individually classify the objects into discrete classes. Discuss problems in determining the number of groups and applying group definitions. Repeat the problem using a more limited set of objects (such as several dark and light shades of lipstick, but leaving out intermediate shades).

3. Present the "racial" classification system used by the U.S. Census and have students critique it in terms of its biological validity.

Multiple-Choice Questions

Correct answers are marked with an asterisk (*). There are multiple questions for certain topics.

1. The reaction between antigens and antibodies allows a person's _____ to be determined.
   *a. blood type
   b. mitochondrial DNA
   c. skin color
   d. dermatoglyphics

2. A person whose blood reacts to the anti-A antibody has blood type
   a. A.
   b. B.
   c. O.
   *d. A or AB.

3. Electrophoresis allows determination of _____ variants.
   a. blood type
   b. mitochondrial DNA
   *c. protein
   d. dermatoglyphic

4. RFLPs are genetic traits that are based on
   a. antigen-antibody reaction.
   b. a person's blood type.
   *c. the length of DNA fragments.
   d. electrophoresis.

5. Measurements of the body, head, and face are known as
   a. dermatoglyphics.
   b. odontometrics.
   c. genetic marker analysis.
   *d. anthropometrics.

6. Anthropologists measure skin color by
   a. restriction fragment length polymorphisms.
   b. antigen-antibody reactions.
   *c. measuring the amount of light reflected off of the skin.
   d. comparing skin color to a series of colored tiles.

7. The study of fingerprints is known as
   a. anthropometrics.
   b. odontometrics.
   *c. dermatoglyphics.
   d. electrophoresis.

8. The measurement of teeth is known as
   a. anthropometrics.
   *b. odontometrics.
   c. dermatoglyphics.
   d. electrophoresis.

9. Anthropologists today agree that there are _____ races in the human species.
    a. 3
    b. 5
    c. 9
   *d. no set number of

10. From a *biological* standpoint, the concept of race is flawed because
    a. people often discriminate against others because of their race.
   *b. much biological variation is continuous.
    c. different races have distinctly different skin colors.
    d. All of the above.

11. Studies of genetic variation within and between traditional "races" shows that _____ percent of total genetic variation occurs between "races."
    a. 0
   *b. 10
    c. 50
    d. 100

12. The frequency of the *O* allele for the ABO blood group system is 0.68 in the San of South Africa and 0.72 in Scotland. Assume you know a particular person has type O blood and that they came from either South Africa or Scotland. What can you tell about that person?
    a. The person must be from Scotland, since the frequency of *O* is higher in Scotland than among the San.
    b. The person is most likely San, but we can't be sure.
    c. The person is most likely from Scotland, but we can't be sure.
   *d. There is no way to tell where this person came from.

13. Skin color in human beings
   *a. is continuous in distribution.
    b. appears in three basic "colors."
    c. appears in five basic "colors."
    d. appears in between three and seven basic "colors," but the exact number is not yet clear.

14. The relatively easy identification of "blacks" and "whites" in the United States reflects the fact that
    a. races are distinct units that are easily determined.
    b. there has been a great deal of natural selection for different skin colors in the United States over the past four centuries.
    *c. the earliest settlers came from regions with different skin colors.
    d. there are relatively few "interracial" marriages.

15. _____ and _____ are both expected to have the same effect on all genetic traits.
    a. Mutation / natural selection
    *b. Genetic drift / gene flow
    c. Genetic drift / natural selection
    d. Mutation / gene flow

16. Imagine three populations: A, B, and C. Suppose you compute the genetic distances and find that the distance between A and B is 2, the distance between A and C is 8, and the distance between B and C is 8. On the basis of these data, population _____ is the most different genetically.
    a. A
    b. B
    *c. C
    d. They are all equally different from one another.

17. What demographic measure would give us an indication of the potential for genetic drift in a population?
    a. migration rates
    b. birth rates
    c. death rates
    *d. population size

18. Which of the following statements regarding IQ test scores is true?
    a. On average, European Americans have higher IQ scores than African Americans.
    b. When educational differences are taken into account, there is no significant difference between European-American and African-American IQ scores.
    c. Poor nutrition can result in lowered IQ scores.
    *d. All of the above.

19. IQ is a measure
    *a. designed initially to identify children with learning disabilities.
    b. of a person's total intelligence.
    c. of a person's worth.
    d. that can be used to sort people into "races."

20. When IQ scores of African Americans were sorted by degree of European ancestry,
    a. those people with greater European ancestry scored higher.
    b. those people with greater African ancestry scored higher.
    *c. there was no relationship.
    d. those people with equal amounts of European and African ancestry scored the highest.

Essay Questions

21. What historical factors are responsible for the appearance of black and white "races" in the United States?

22. What does the relative proportion of variation *between* and *within* human "races" tell us about human variation and the usefulness of the biological race concept?

CHAPTER 11

HUMAN MICROEVOLUTION

Overview

This chapter provides a number of case studies of human microevolution. The first part of the chapter looks at two case studies of gene flow and genetic drift in human populations, with particular emphasis on migration, population size, and cultural behaviors. The second part of the chapter provides several case studies of natural selection in human populations, and concludes with a discussion of developmental acclimatization.

Outline

I.   Case Studies of Gene Flow and Genetic Drift
   A. Social Organization and Genetics of South American Indians of the Rain Forest
   B. The Vikings and Irish Population History

II. Case Studies of Natural Selection
   A. Hemoglobin, Sickle Cell, and Malaria
     1. Hemoglobin variants
     2. Distribution of the sickle cell allele and malaria
     3. Effects of culture change on sickle cell frequency
     4. Other relationships with malaria
   B. The ABO Blood Group and Natural Selection
   C. Lactase Deficiency
   D. Skin Color
     1. The distribution of skin color
     2. Skin cancer, sunburn, and ultraviolet radiation
     3. The vitamin D hypothesis
     4. Skin color and cold injury
   E. Natural Selection or Developmental Acclimatization?
     1. High-altitude adaptation
     2. Body size, body shape, and climate

III. Summary

IV. Supplemental Readings

   Special Topic: The Biological History of the Ancient Egyptians

Topics for Discussion

1. What is the extent of genetic drift expected in a modern urban population? Discuss the number of ways in which societies are subdivided (e.g., social class, religion, ethnicity) and how this subdivision could affect levels of genetic drift.

2. Why do most humans (even today) tend to choose mates from a local geographic area? What is the genetic effect of this behavior?

3. Why is it that the effects of natural selection in human populations may often be so difficult to show but yet have major evolutionary impact?

Multiple-Choice Questions

Correct answers are marked with an asterisk (*). There are multiple questions for certain topics.

1. In human populations, the practice of exogamy acts to
   a. decrease gene flow and increase genetic drift.
   b. decrease gene flow and decrease genetic drift.
   *c. increase gene flow and decrease genetic drift.
   d. increase gene flow and increase genetic drift.

2. When the populations of certain South American native groups become too large, they
   a. experience fusion.
   *b. experience fission.
   c. experience considerable genetic drift.
   d. move to Central America.

3. Studies of genetic drift in South American Indian populations have shown that
   a. changes in group size and composition have little effect on genetic variation.
   *b. groups that fission in a nonrandom manner increase the effect of genetic drift.
   c. genetic drift has little impact given the high degree of natural selection on most loci in these populations.
   d. most South American Indian populations have had considerable European admixture.

4. A study of Irish genetic distances showed genetic distinctiveness of several counties in the midlands of Ireland. This genetic distinctiveness reflects
   *a. gene flow from Vikings in historic times.
   b. balancing selection.
   c. gene flow from England in historic times.
   d. higher mutation rates due to background radiation in this region.

5. Sickle cell anemia occurs in people with the genotype
   a. *AA*
   b. *AS*
   *c. *SS*
   d. All of the above.

6. Which of the following statements regarding the sickle cell allele is true?
   a. The frequency of the allele is *higher* than the frequency of the normal hemoglobin allele in many African populations.
   b. The frequency of the allele in African Americans has *increased* since the colonization of the United States.
   *c. The frequency of the sickle cell allele is *higher* in malarial regions than in non-malarial regions.
   d. None of the above.

7. Which genotype has the highest fitness in a malarial environment?
   *a. *AA*
   b. *AS*
   c. *SS*
   d. They all have equal fitness.

8. Which genotype has the highest fitness in an environment *without* malaria?
   *a. *AA*
   b. *AS*
   c. *SS*
   d. They all have equal fitness.

9. The relationship between sickle cell allele frequencies and malaria provides an excellent example of selection
   a. against the recessive homozygote.
   b. for the recessive homozygote.
   c. against the heterozygote.
   *d. for the heterozygote.

10. A rise in the mosquito population among some African populations had resulted from environmental changes brought about by
    *a. horticulture.
    b. urbanization.
    c. irrigation.
    d. increased pollution.

11. Studies have found evidence of a link between ABO blood group phenotypes and
    a. infectious disease.
    b. noninfectious disease.
    c. maternal-fetal incompatibility.
    *d. All of the above.

12. Worldwide, the most common allele for the ABO system is
    a. *A*.
    b. *B*.
    *c. *O*.
    d. They all have the same frequency.

13. The frequency of the *B* allele for the ABO blood group is high in India, perhaps reflecting
    *a. selection due to smallpox and plague.
    b. European gene flow.
    c. mutation.
    d. preferential inbreeding.

14. A pregnancy with Rhesus maternal-fetal incompatibility *and* ABO maternal-fetal incompatibility is
    a. just as harmful as being Rhesus-incompatible alone.
    *b. less harmful than being incompatible for only one (Rhesus or ABO).
    c. always fatal.
    d. not genetically possible.

15. Lower frequencies of lactase deficiency tend to be found in populations
    a. that live in malarial environments.
    *b. that rely heavily on dairy farming.
    c. that live at high altitudes.
    d. that have experienced epidemics of smallpox.

16. People that are lactase deficient
    a. are always African, although not all Africans are lactase deficient.
    b. are less susceptible to malaria.
    *c. have difficulty digesting milk sugar after the first few years of their life.
    d. never survive until adulthood.

17. The major pigment responsible for skin color variation is
    a. hemoglobin.
    b. carotene.
    *c. melanin
    d. None of the above.

18. The pink hue of "white" people results from the _____ pigment.
    *a. hemoglobin.
    b. carotene.
    c. melanin
    d. None of the above.

19. Dark skinned individuals are at _____ near the equator because their skin color _____.
    *a. an advantage / prevents skin cancer and sunburn
    b. a disadvantage / leads to increased frostbite
    c. an advantage / allows increased production of vitamin D
    d. a disadvantage / reduces vitamin D production

20. Contrary to the "vitamin D hypothesis," studies of vitamin D production among people living in rural northern climates show that
    a. dark-skinned peoples produce too much vitamin D.
    *b. dark-skinned peoples produce sufficient vitamin D.
    c. dark-skinned peoples produce too little vitamin D.
    d. light-skinned peoples produce too much vitamin D.

21. The "vitamin D hypothesis" held that dark skin would be at a disadvantage in northern climates, since the lack of vitamin D would lead to
    a. malaria.
    b. smallpox.
    *c. rickets.
    d. malnutrition.

22. Studies of soldiers during the Korean War suggest that dark-skinned people are more prone to _____ than light-skinned people.
    a.   sickle cell anemia
    b.   vitamin D deficiency
    *c.   frostbite
    d.   liver cancer

23. Studies of the skulls of ancient Egyptians shows that they were biologically most similar to
    a.   East Asians.
    b.   sub-Saharan Africans.
    c.   Europeans.
    *d.   None of the above.

24. Developmental acclimatization is
    a.   short-term physiologic adaptation.
    b.   long-term physiologic adaptation.
    *c.   long-term adaptation that occurs during physical growth.
    d.   genetic adaptation (natural selection).

25. Larger body mass is adaptive in
    *a.   cold climates.
    b.   hot climates.
    c.   high-altitude environments.
    d.   malarial environments.

26. A linear body shape is adaptive in
    a.   cold climates.
    *b.   hot climates.
    c.   high-altitude environments.
    d.   malarial environments.

27. Individuals with shorter and bulkier limbs are more adaptive in
    *a.   cold climates.
    b.   hot climates.
    c.   high-altitude environments.
    d.   malarial environments.

28. Studies of the relationship between climate and body size and shape have shown that, on average, individuals with _____ and _____ are better suited to a hot climate.
    a.   small body mass / less linear body shape.
    *b.   small body mass / linear body shape.
    c.   large body mass / less linear body shape.
    d.   large body mass / linear body shape.

29. Hypoxia is
   *a. oxygen starvation.
   b. nutritional stress.
   c. a rare form of sickle cell anemia.
   d. another name for smallpox.

30. Hypoxia is a stress that occurs in _____ environments.
   a. cold
   *b. high-altitude
   c. hot and dry
   d. hot and wet

31. Some populations show increased chest dimensions, reflecting adaptation to a _____ environment.
   a. equatorial
   b. cold and dry
   c. cold and wet
   *d. high-altitude

32. What is the relationship between adaptation to a high-altitude environment and the age at which someone migrates into that environment?
   a. The older you are when you move, the more you adapt.
   *b. The younger you are when you move, the more you adapt.
   c. Adaptation can only occur if migration takes place in the first year of life.
   d. There is no relationship.

33. Recent studies of human growth in high-altitude environments show that _____ is a major factor leading to reduced height in some high-altitude populations.
   a. cold stress
   *b. poor nutrition
   c. infectious disease
   d. heat stress

Essay Questions

34. In many European agricultural populations, it is common for only one son from a large family to marry and have children. How might this cultural pattern affect the degree of genetic drift in such societies?

35. Describe one study of natural selection that shows the influence of culture change. Be specific.

36. Describe briefly the different hypotheses for the origin of lighter skin in humans that have lived further from the equator.

37. What is the relationship between human body size and shape and average temperature? Explain the physiologic reasons for this relationship in terms of mammalian biology.

CHAPTER 12

HUMAN BIOLOGY AND CULTURE CHANGE

Overview

This chapter examines the changing patterns of human biology and how it relates to culture change during human evolution and in today's world. The chapter begins with a discussion of changes in health and disease that have accompanied the culture changes from hunting and gathering to agricultural to industrialization. This section includes discussion of the transition to agriculture, the biological impact of culture contact, the epidemiologic transition, and secular changes in human growth. The final section of the chapter looks at demographic change in relation to culture change, with particular emphasis on the changing demographic patterns in today's world.

Outline

I.   The Evolution of Human Disease
   A. Disease in Hunting-Gathering Societies
      1. Infectious disease
      2. Noninfectious disease
      3. Other causes of death
   B. Agriculture and Disease
      1. Infectious disease
      2. Nutritional disease
   C. Urbanization and Disease
      1. Disease in preindustrial cities
      2. Disease in industrial cities
   D. Culture Contact
   E. The Epidemiologic Transition
      1. The nature of the epidemiologic transition
      2. Studies of the epidemiologic transition
   F. Secular Changes in Human Growth
      1. Types of secular changes
      2. Causes of secular change
   G. Some Contemporary Issues
      1. The "New World syndrome"
      2. AIDS
      3. Protein-calorie malnutrition

II. The Demographic Evolution of Human Populations
    A. The Study of Demography
        1. Demographic measures
        2. Population growth
        3. The age-sex structure of populations
    B. Demography and the Modern World
        1. The demographic transition
        2. World population growth
        3. Implications of changing age structure

III. Summary

IV. Supplemental Readings

    Special Topic: The Coming Plague?
    Special Topic: The Baby Boom

Topics for Discussion

1. Discuss how the shift from infectious diseases to noninfectious diseases as leading causes of death, and the increase in life expectancy, are changing our society's approach to solving health problems.

2. Present a case study from an epidemiology or medical anthropology text and have the class work through the problems in inferring disease causation and spread.

3. Discuss how disease affects cultural values and behaviors. Two good examples are the Black Death and AIDS.

4. Discuss Kenneth Weiss' paper "On the number of the genus *Homo* who have ever lived, and some evolutionary implications" (*Human Biology* 56:637–649, 1984).

5. Discuss potential impacts of changing age structure in the United States, especially in terms of health care and Social Security programs.

Multiple-Choice Questions

Correct answers are marked with an asterisk (*). There are multiple questions for certain topics.

1. A _____ disease is one caused by microorganisms and that can be spread directly from one person to another.
   a. noncommunicable noninfectious
   b. noncommunicable infectious
   c. communicable noninfectious
   *d. communicable infectious

2. _____ pattern is one where diseases occur at a low but constant rate in a population.
   a. A transitional
   b. A pandemic
   c. An epidemic
   *d. An endemic

3. A pandemic is
   *a. a widespread epidemic, often affecting entire continents.
   b. a localized epidemic, usually affecting only individuals within a few miles.
   c. an initial outbreak of a communicable infectious disease.
   d. an epidemic that lasts more than a single human generation.

4. Plots of death rates in the twentieth century from around the world tend to peak in the year 1918. What happened?
   *a. a worldwide flu pandemic
   b. a worldwide pandemic of bubonic plague
   c. the evolution of venereal syphilis from a relatively harmless skin disease
   d. the first use of chemical warfare during World War I

5. Pandemics
   a. include the bubonic plague pandemic of the Middle Ages.
   b. include the 1918 flu pandemic.
   c. still occur in the world today.
   *d. All of the above.

6. Zoonoses are diseases that
   a. are epidemics in zoos.
   b. are quite common in cities.
   *c. are transmitted from other animals to humans.
   d. never affect humans.

7. One of the major causes of death in many hunting and gathering societies is
    a. cancer.
    b. epidemic infectious diseases.
   *c. injury.
    d. starvation.

8. Hunting and gathering populations are prone to _____ infectious diseases.
    a. frequent epidemic
   *b. endemic
    c. occasional epidemic
    d. pandemic

9. Noninfectious disease, such as heart disease and cancer, is _____ in hunting and gathering populations, compared to the United States.
    a. somewhat more common
    b. equally as common
   *c. rare
    d. much more common

10. In general, the nutritional quality of hunting and gathering populations is
    a. poor.
    b. fair to good.
   *c. excellent.
    d. unknown.

11. Life expectancy at birth in hunting and gathering populations is generally _____ years.
   *a. 20 to 40
    b. 40 to 50
    c. 50 to 60
    d. 75

12. What will happen to life expectancy at birth if there is an increase in *infant* mortality?
   *a. It will decrease.
    b. It will stay the same.
    c. It will increase.
    d. Unknown.

13. Infectious diseases are most likely to become epidemic in
    _____ populations.
    a. small nomadic
    b. large nomadic
    c. small sedentary
    *d. large sedentary

14. _____ has been eliminated worldwide.
    a. Malaria
    b. Tuberculosis
    c. Measles
    *d. Smallpox

15. Epidemics of diseases such as smallpox and measles *first* became
    common in _____ populations.
    a. hunting and gathering
    *b. agricultural
    c. early urban
    d. modern urban

16. Compared to hunting and gathering populations, the nutritional
    quality of early agricultural populations was
    *a. worse.
    b. about the same.
    c. better.
    d. unknown.

17. Dental problems became more common with the development of
    _____ populations.
    a. hunting and gathering
    *b. agricultural
    c. early urban
    d. modern urban

18. The transition from hunting and gathering to agriculture was
    accompanied by an increase in
    a. nutritional stress.
    b. infectious disease.
    c. dental decay.
    *d. All of the above.

19. Severe epidemics occurred in preindustrial cities because of
    a. high population size and density.
    b. a lack of sanitation.
    c. contaminated water.
    *d. All of the above.

20. The culture contact that resulted following European exploration in the 1500s resulted in diseases being exchanged between the Old World and the New World. The flow of disease was
   a. roughly equal in both directions.
   b. primarily from the New World to the Old World.
   *c. primarily from the Old World to the New World.
   d. primarily from Australia to Hawaii.

21. At present, the bulk of the evidence from paleopathology suggests that syphilis originated
   *a. in the New World.
   b. in the Old World.
   c. simultaneously throughout the world.
   d. in Europe during the last 100 years.

22. What impact has the development of sewers and clean water had on infectious diseases?
   *a. They were primarily responsible for the epidemiologic transition.
   b. No effect at all.
   c. The development of sewer systems *increased* the spread of disease organisms.
   d. Some effect, but not as much as improved nutrition.

23. Which of the following is *not* a characteristic of the epidemiologic transition?
   *a. There has been an *increase* in *both* life span and life expectancy.
   b. There has been a *decrease* in infectious disease.
   c. There has been an *increase* in noninfectious disease.
   d. The major causes of death have changed.

24. The maximum *life span* (not life expectancy) of human beings is _____ years.
   a. 50
   b. 75
   c. 100
   *d. 120

25. Life expectancy at birth in the United States today is roughly _____ years.
   a. 50
   b. 65
   *c. 75
   d. 120

26. The epidemiologic transition has resulted in _____ in the rate of infectious disease and _____ in the rate of noninfectious disease.
    a. a decrease / a decrease
    *b. a decrease / an increase
    c. an increase / a decrease
    d. an increase / an increase

27. An increase in the rate of cancers in the United States over the past century is primarily due to
    a. changes in the physical environment (e.g., increased pollution).
    b. changes in classification of diseases.
    *c. people living longer (thus having time to get cancer).
    d. an increase in immigration.

28. One example of a secular change is that average _____ has *decreased* during the last century in Western societies.
    a. height
    b. weight
    c. brain size
    *d. age at menarche

29. Which of the following is a characteristic of secular trend in human growth?
    *a. Improved health can lead to an increase in maximum adult height.
    b. Improved nutrition has no effect on maximum adult height.
    c. Adult height differs by religious affiliation.
    d. Changes in adult height are primarily due to decreased genetic drift.

30. Compared to children 100 years ago, the average child (of the same age) in the United States today is
    *a. taller and heavier.
    b. taller and lighter.
    c. shorter and heavier.
    d. shorter and lighter.

31. Age at menarche is the age
    a. when the adolescent growth spurt occurs in males.
    b. when the adolescent growth spurt occurs in females.
    *c. at which a female experiences her first menstrual period.
    d. at which secondary sexual characteristics appear.

32. Secular changes are caused by
    a. improved nutrition.
    b. reduction in childhood infectious disease.
    c. improved standard of living.
    *d. All of the above.

33. The "New World syndrome" refers to higher rates of
    _____ among people of Native American ancestry.
    *a. certain non-infectious disorders
    b. smallpox and measles
    c. infertility
    d. motor vehicle injuries

34. Among Mexican Americans, diabetes is most frequent in those
    individuals with _____ ancestry.
    a. more African
    b. less African
    *c. more Native American
    d. less Native American

35. The group most likely to acquire AIDS in the United States today
    is
    a. male intravenous drug users.
    b. female intravenous drug users.
    c. men who have sex with women.
    *d. men who have sex with other men.

36. Kwashiorkor and marasmus are
    a. sites where archaic *Homo sapiens* fossils have been
       discovered.
    b. examples of pandemic infectious diseases.
    *c. protein-calorie malnutrition diseases.
    d. diseases that spread from the Old World to the New World
       following European contact.

37. What is a reasonable prediction about the future of infectious
    disease?
    a. Infectious diseases will almost all disappear in the near
       future.
    *b. We must be on guard for microorganisms that evolve
       resistance to antibiotics.
    c. The current types and rates of diseases will remain the same
       as today.
    d. We will be extinct within a decade.

38. Fecundity refers to
    a. the actual number of children that are born.
    b. the actual number of conceptions taking place.
    *c. the number of people capable of having children.
    d. the total number of infants in a population.

39. In human populations, mortality rates are generally highest among _____ and, secondarily, among _____.
    *a. the elderly / infants
    b. infants / the elderly
    c. infants / teenagers
    d. the elderly / teenagers

40. In human populations, mortality rates are highest among
    a. infants.
    b. teenagers.
    c. the middle-aged.
    *d. the elderly.

41. Natural increase refers to
    *a. births minus deaths.
    b. births minus deaths, plus or minus migration.
    c. the total number of births.
    d. births plus migration.

42. Assuming no migration, population growth occurs when
    *a. birth rates are greater than death rates.
    b. birth rates are equal to death rates.
    c. birth rates are less than death rates.
    d. birth rates are zero.

43. Carrying capacity refers to
    a. the maximum physical work of an average person.
    b. the number of game herds in a region.
    *c. the population size an environment can support.
    d. the ratio of farmers to non-farmers in an agricultural society.

44. Compared to *developing* nations, the age structure of *developed* nations shows
    a. a greater proportion of infants and a greater proportion of the elderly.
    b. a greater proportion of infants and a smaller proportion of the elderly.
    *c. a smaller proportion of infants and a greater proportion of the elderly.
    d. a smaller proportion of infants and a smaller proportion of the elderly.

45. Demographic transition theory states that *developed* nations (such as the United States) typically have _____ fertility rates and _____ mortality rates.
    a. high / high
    b. high /low
    *c. low / low
    d. low / high

46. According to the demographic transition theory
    *a. death rates *decline* first, followed by a *decline* in birth rates.
    b. birth rates *decline* first, followed by a *decline* in death rates.
    c. birth and death rates both *decline* at the same time.
    d. birth rates and death rates both *increase* at the same time.

47. The world population is now close to _____ billion people.
    a. 1
    b. 3
    *c. 6
    d. 12

48. The rapid increase in fertility in the United States between 1946 and 1964 (the "Baby Boom") was due to
    a. laws prohibiting contraceptive devices among unmarried people.
    *b. improved economic conditions resulting in earlier marriage and larger families.
    c. the return of soldiers from World War II.
    d. massive unemployment.

Essay Questions

49. What is the epidemiologic transition? What are its stages? What are its causes?

50. What are the ecological reasons that epidemics of infectious disease are more common in agricultural populations than in hunting-gathering populations?

51. What is a secular change in human growth? What are the major secular changes that have occurred in developed nations during the past century? What are the causes of these secular changes?

52. What impact can culture contact have on disease? Give a specific example.

53. Why did the birth rate in the U.S. increase after World War II?

54. Describe briefly demographic transition theory, and the effect of a demographic transition on population growth and age structure.

Sources for Laboratory Equipment

The following is a partial list of sources for human and nonhuman primate skeletal material (S), fossil casts (F), and materials for genetics experiments (G).

Carolina Biological Supply Co.   (S, F, G)
2700 York Road
Burlington, NC 27215
(800) 334-5551

Casting Department   (F)
National Museums of Kenya
P.O. Box 40658
Nairobi, Kenya

Casting Program   (F)
Department of Anthropology
University of Pennsylvania
Philadelphia, PA 19104

France Casting   (S)
Diane L. France, Ph.D.
20102 Buckhorn Road
Bellvue, CO 80512
(303) 221-4044

Ward's Natural Science Establishment, Inc.   (S, F, G)
5100 West Henrietta Road
P.O. Box 92912
Rochester, NY 14692-9012
(800) 962-2660